The Witch's Book of Wisdom

The Witch's Book of Wisdom

PATRICIA TELESCO

CITADEL PRESS
Kensington Publishing Corp.
www.kensingtonbooks.com

CITADEL PRESS books are published by
Kensington Publishing Corp.
850 Third Avenue
New York, NY 10022

All Kensington titles, imprints, and distributed lines are available at
special quantity discounts for bulk purchases for sales promotions,
premiums, fund-raising, educational, or institutional use. Special book
excerpts or customized printings can also be created to fit specific needs.
For details, write or phone the office of the Kensington special sales
manager: Kensington Publishing Corp., 850 Third Avenue, New York,
NY 10022, attn: Special Sales Department; phone 1-800-221-2647.

CITADEL PRESS and the Citadel logo are Reg. U.S. Pat. & TM Off.

First printing: August 2003
10 9 8 7 6 5 4 3 2 1

Printed in the United States of America

Library of Congress Control Number: 2002116579
ISBN 0-8065-2411-1

With thanks to the elders, teachers, and leaders in the neo-Pagan community, who serve with both heart and hand and have helped me repeatedly to keep my feet on the path of beauty.

Contents

Preface

Wisdom outweighs strength.   —African Proverb

Real wisdom comes from self-realization.   —Chew Nai Chee

Even a hundred years ago, an individual could often go to his or her village wise person for mundane and magickal advice on everything from finding love and improving finances to healing cattle! Now our proverbial "village" has grown dramatically, and with that growth has come a variety of societal and economic adjustments. Even so, while only a few of us own cattle (more often than not it's a pet cat), we are not that different from our ancestors. We still yearn for love, financial security, and sound spiritual guidance.

Unfortunately for those of us walking the Path of alternative religions, it's rare to find words like *Witch, Cunning Folk,* or *High Priest/ess* listed anywhere in the local Yellow Pages! And, quite honestly, you probably wouldn't want to seek out a metaphysical advisor from classified ads anyway. The New Age movement, like so many social swells, has become "big business." This business has its fair share of moneychangers looking for a piece of the pie generated by hungry spiritual seekers. So how can anyone, especially the solitary practitioner, find a trusted individual to turn to for important insights and help?

That's where *The Witch's Book Of Wisdom* begins! The entire purpose of this book is to provide a nurturing, sound, practical, and fun-loving outlook on magick and spirituality as they intertwine with your everyday life. When you find yourself looking for a good ear or wise words, come to these pages and explore the lessons and insights I've gathered over eighteen years of magickal practice into this writing, not to mention the tidbits of wisdom that friends and teachers have shared with me, and that lodged in my heart.

As you read, please know it's not my desire to become some kind of guru, just a fellow traveler who hopes to help make the way less long and less hard for others. In looking back, perhaps the most important lesson for me in recent years has been quite simple: We need each other. We need a family, a community, a tribe, or some other form of connection through which to feed our souls. In this case, the kinship is generated from the pages of a book, but that doesn't lessen the importance of the connection.

Consider—perhaps I have successfully been through something similar to what you're experiencing. Or, perhaps I posed similar questions to a wise person in my travels as those questions you have on your mind right now (you know, the nagging ones that wake you up at 3 A.M.). If I found resolutions, and received good answers, then why should you have to reinvent the wheel or start from scratch? While there is certainly value in bravely figuring everything out on your own, there's nothing that says you can't review tried-and-true advice and perspectives.

Throughout my spiritual quest I've experienced dismal failures, faced joys and sorrows, and generally discovered that the more I know, the more I realize how much I've yet to learn! And I remember how many times I wished I had a friend or book like this one to help with the more difficult moments. If this sounds familiar, you're not alone. Every sincere seeker comes to that very same point if they're being wholly honest with self and Spirit. It is a very good place to be because it's balanced between reality and hope, the mundane and metaphysical, the ordinary and the miraculous!

With this delicate balance in mind, *The Witch's Book Of Wisdom* begins by reviewing the role of the village wise person and how that role evolved with various cultures and eras. After all, the tradition of accessible, realistic advice that Cunning People provided is the cornerstone of this book. Getting a peek at a day in the life of such individuals, and their amazing importance to many communities, is nothing short of inspirational. It speaks strongly of what any magickal practitioner or group could become in their communities with a little elbow grease, good intentions, and some productive networking.

Going one step further *The Witch's Book of Wisdom* covers a wide variety of subjects that lay heavily on many people's hearts. Whether it's perspectives for dating or dumping, instructions for making a proactive protection potion, guidelines for a luck-inspiring charm, sample spells to silence gossip, or a ritual for righteous indignation, *The Witch's Book of Wisdom* isn't afraid to tackle sensitive issues and tell it like it is.

I am a firm believer in the keep-it-simple-shoot-from-the-hip school of spirituality. It is long past time that we stopped trying to put words like *witch* and *pagan* in the same sentence with political correctness. It simply doesn't work. It is also long past time we stopped shying away from a realistic portrait of who we (Pagans, Wiccans, Druids, Shamans, etc.) are as a whole, celebrating both our differences and similarities. Until we do this, the world as a whole cannot begin to truly accept emerging faiths as something transformational, potent, and permanent.

Now, before this proverbial "Granny GoodWitch" with a sly tongue puts you off, bear in mind that these soulful servings of frankness are balanced with an equal measure of humor, compassion, and whimsy. The goal here is keeping things down to earth, realistic, pragmatic, and immediately useful in the challenging and sometimes overwhelming 9 to 5 world you face daily. In fact, in the honored tradition of hedge witchery and Cunning Folk, the components suggested throughout *A Witch's Book of Wisdom* are all readily available around the sacred space of home or at a nearby store. The processes provided are not overly time consuming, nor do they smack of Hollywood hocus-pocus. The sample incantations and invocations are written in street English—not a *thee, thou,* or *doth* to be found! Throughout this book, practicality, playfulness, positive outlooks, and a healthy dose of personal vision create the foundation for meaningful and empowering results. Which brings me to an important point.

My words are not carved in stone. I am a simple folk magician who struggles daily with the way, the Path, the uncertainties, and the ethics of our beliefs. All I can hope to do is share with you honestly from the light that I have. To these humble words, please bring your own vision and experiences. Ultimately the personalization process yields far more satisfying results than precontrived structures. Tweak the phrasing of the spells, fiddle with the recipes, rewrite the rituals, and blend the blessings until they truly sing with the song of your Higher Self.

Bright and beautiful blessings be yours.

Prologue:
Archetype of the Wise Person

Skill to do comes of doing.   —Ralph Waldo Emerson

*Do not believe in anything simply because you have heard it. Do not be-
lieve in anything simply because it is spoken and rumored by many. Do
not believe in anything simply because it is found written in your religious books. Do not believe in anything merely on the authority of your
teachers and elders. Do not believe in traditions because they have been
handed down for many generations. But after observation and analysis,
when you find that anything agrees with reason and is conducive to the
good and benefit of one and all, then accept it and live up to it.*

—Buddha

WHEN I THINK OF A VILLAGE WISE PERSON, MY MIND WAN-
ders to a remote place on the edge of the woods. There, a man or
woman stands surrounded by animals and harvested herbs, concocting
something in an iron pot over a well-tended hearth fire. This person
lives alone by choice, their only company being nature and the love of
the work. Perhaps this image is romanticized, but it is part of what has
become an archetype in the metaphysical movement as surely as that of
a Druid or Shaman.

Why consider it an archetype? Because it's an image to which many

1

Wiccans and neo-Pagans point as being a prototype that expresses the heart and soul of where we've come from historically. It is also a positive role model for where magickal lifestyles may go in the future. Living close to the land (or at least being respectful of the Earth), being skilled in our arts, helping our communities, and being at peace with self and Spirit are worthy treasures to gather from this simple but sublime portrait. But I'm getting ahead of myself.

In exploring the legacy of the Cunning Person, I've relied mostly on European history, as that's where this archetype seems to appear regularly. It is quite certain that other cultures had expressions of this type, too, but they achieved little more than passing mention in history books. It was simply common knowledge that any reasonably sized village would likely house a healer, a Shaman, a wise person, or someone similar to serve the locale.

So what set apart the Cunning Folk from everyday "Joes" and how did they become known in their communities? The most important factor seems to be that Cunning Folk and wise people were often literate and were among the first of the "common" people to keep effective herbal and magickal formulas written down. Cornelius Agrippa's *Occult Philosophy*, while more geared toward High Magick, is filled with sound examples of medicinals, rituals, spells, and astrological data collected from prevalent contemporary folk wisdom (in this case "contemporary" meaning the late 1400s). Quite literally, you can find here everything from helping birth a calf to healing a broken heart.

It was this type of immediately applicable knowledge and skill that endeared the Cunning Folk to the hearts of villagers and kings alike. So much was it the case that, historically speaking, the Cunning Folk were rarely accused of being witches. The need for healers and good advisors apparently overcame some of the fears and superstitions associated with the wise person's magickal ways!

The reasons a person would go to the village wise person for consultation varied greatly. Some sought help finding a lost item or the name of a thief, others needed healing salves for a farm animal, and others still requested spells or charms for themselves or family members. Beyond this the Cunning Person's duties were highly diversified, ranging from curing the sick and encouraging love to designing spells for bountiful crop growth and providing protective amulets. The methods and tools central to all this charming, blessing, conjuring, and seeing true came from magickal, familial, and cultural folklore and practices.

Mind you, magick wasn't the only thing touted in the Cunning Person's kit. Typically these people blended potions and notions while dispensing heaping helpings of old-fashioned common sense too (which is rarely *common!*). Why work several spells when encouraging words and a hug would do the trick? This is among the most important lessons of this archetype. Magick was never intended to fix all of life's problems; it's a helpmate. First, see what you can do by employing a little forethought, or by working toward goals with your hands, mind, and heart fully engaged. If the mundane efforts fall short or need support, then go to the metaphysical ones. This process supports the idea of each person being a cocreator who stands at the helm of his or her destiny.

Regardless of the era or cultural setting, humankind turned to Cunning People again and again for spiritual development and assistance. Anthropologists believe, because of this universality, that the Cunning Folk tended toward religious neutrality, except where circumstances created a necessity. For example, when we examine the wording of the remaining spells and incantations of European folk healers we discover them calling upon archangels, using Latin prayers, and blending in components that had prevalent religious symbolism. This way the wise person could work side-by-side with "mainstream" priests for the good of the community, utilizing all the mental, physical, and spiritual tools in his or her kit. In this respect, Priests and Cunning Folk became the first psychologists and counselors.

The Cunning Person's neutrality implies that the wisdom of these people was what Aristotle classified as an intellectual virtue. While we think of our ancestors as very simple people, they nevertheless were not lacking in what we now call "street smarts." The only way a Cunning Person could be truly valued by a community (from whom they would then get sustenance via traded goods) was to serve without prejudice within the limits of human failings. Unfortunately, this also led to a number of wise people being run out of town or killed by those who felt that the unilateral application of cunning arts somehow undermined those in authority (or the authority figures found displeasure in those individuals the cunning person chose to help).

Thus we see a second good lesson here. As humans there are limits to our ability to remain wholly neutral, and indeed we can't always do so without breaking personal or professional ethics. Modern Cunning Folk must serve communities while remaining aware of their personal humanness. They must also serve with an awareness of the prevalent pressures, politics, and circumstances prevailing in that community. In short, sometimes the most well-meaning witch in the world must trust himself or herself enough to say no, for the greater good.

A third lesson gleaned from this brief review is the adaptable nature of the Cunning Person archetype. While some methods from these people remain intact in their original form, other parts have been adapted to emerging customs and social structure. For example, Druids used to honor tree spirits. Later in history this practice transformed into healers using twin tree branches as a symbolic medium through which to pass a patient (implying movement from sickness to health), or they might "attach" a malady to a tree and leave it there, via a piece of a patient's clothing. (There are a lot more ways in which trees figured into the Cunning Person's art, but you get the idea.) Today, however, we simply knock on wood for improved fortune without worshipping the tree, and usually without having any notion of where this custom originated. The power in the tradition endured because it was allowed to change as societal and cultural transformations dictated, otherwise it might have been lost to a pyre!

Beyond this adaptability we find a knack for multitasking. The Cunning Arts were never limited to just herbalism or any other specific practice. Rather history paints the image of the wise person as a generalist with a few key talents. These talents have a vast range, and might include anything from wort cunning, animal ken, weather magick, and hedge witchery to kitchen magick, love potions, curses, green magick, and divination. In this manner the Cunning Folk passed down a respect for diversity, creativity, and tradition to future generations. It is a heritage from which the modern neo-Pagan movement seems to derive many of its patterns and prototypes.

One rather interesting note to this historical survey is the discovery that a great number of Cunning Folk were not just the stereotypical old woman. Some were young women or men of various ages. Even though we use the phrase "wise woman" frequently in contemporary language, it would be shortsighted to limit our exploration to only that gender. In some instances the women practicing as village witches were single by choice or death of a mate. This was one way of avoiding the usual social stigma associated with her choice, by proving that she need not be wed to another family member to provide for herself. Alternatively, a man or woman may have been thrust into carrying on a tradition after his or her teacher died (the townspeople already being dependent on that reliable fixture). This was especially true if that teacher was the man or woman's parent or grandparent.

As for the men specifically practicing this tradition, it's interesting to notice that they kept their spells secret and protected their craft from "witches," whom they labeled as wilder and more malevolent. Whether these men used such descriptions to protect themselves from potential persecution is unknown, but it seems highly likely. Nonetheless, this (along with the prevalence of male High Magicians) helps unravel the veil hung over witchcraft and Cunning Arts as being simply a woman's fancy!

I mention this issue of gender because in the modern magickal movement there still seems to be some misunderstanding of the term *witch* as applying to men and women equally. In our times it is nongender specific (even if it wasn't always depicted as such historically). Additionally, the ratio of men and women practitioners is slowly, but steadily, balancing out. Men are rediscovering their medicine and magick, and should know that they too have a rich legacy on which to build.

In summary, the following are the key components to the Cunning Folk archetype as explored in this book:

- The ability to adapt to present and future circumstances and ideals without losing sight of custom and its importance

- The blending of spiritual methods and ideals with daily life in practical and functional ways

- The skillful and dependable application of one's knowledge and training to meet everyday needs

- A determined diversification of skills so as to better adapt and serve

- The collection, preservation, and honoring of tradition

- The application of common sense (e.g., hard work is still good magick)

- Maintaining an ongoing awareness of responsibility to self (ethics) and the community one serves

- An appreciation for, and reverence toward, nature's gifts, symbols, and signs

- A respect for titles as being representative of a level of achievement, but also knowing that a title means nothing if one does not "walk the walk"

- Release of gender-specific expectations in this art or any aspect of life

To my thinking these are good components to integrate into any positive spiritual Path, not just the Cunning Arts.

Everything Old Is New Again

With these tidbits from the history of Cunning Arts in mind, we can now look at our reality today. As mentioned in the preface, our "village" has gone global. We can now literally reach across the world in seconds with information and knowledge. However, with matters that touch our very souls, we don't necessarily want to trust a stranger or an unknown website!

This reality set me to thinking about how a modern Cunning Person could best help the magickal community. We can certainly begin in our own proverbial backyards, as did our ancestors. We can also gather and honor our ancestor's lessons and insights so long as we apply them gently to this brave new world in which we live. But that still doesn't answer the prevailing issues facing numerous solitary practitioners, or those who are a long way from home and in need of help.

In part, the worldwide web fills some of the gaps that naturally develop in a mobile society. We can get online, check out chats, browse magickal bulletin boards, gather with e-groups, and cruise around cyber covens. Yet these still lack the personal touch. Then, too, there are always old-fashioned phone calls and snail mail! No matter what, by staying in touch with people you know and respect for their input, you honor them and help maintain an ongoing network of "village" wise persons that we can reach quickly.

And for the rest, if you don't have someone nearby to turn to, or even if you just want an extra resource with alternative vantage points, I leave you in good hands with the pages of this book. While there is no way one tome could come close to touching on all the matters of spiritual and mundane life (that would require a multivolume encyclopedia), every effort has been made to broach the more important ones. It is my fervent prayer that somehow my efforts here will help you today, tomorrow, and long into the future. If after reading you find you have a nagging question that isn't answered herein, just e-mail me at Granny@loresinger.com. I will answer you as quickly as possible, with as much information as I have to offer.

Now, let's get down to business!

Granny GoodWitch Says...

Using This Book

Applying this book is really quite simple. Think of a topic about which you'd like to learn more or gain some alternative insights. Boil down your musings to a one-word theme (like health, love, protection, etc.). Look up that word in these alphabetized listings and read over the materials and activities. Don't stop there, however! Meditate on the ideas, try (or adapt) the exercises, and then decide what you will apply as truth and what is "good" for your life and reality.

Now there are going to be topics that may not be listed here, and some that cross over into more than one category. In the case of the former, think synonyms. For example, *money* crosses over into *jobs* and *employment*. If you're worried about keeping your money safe or making sound investments, try the topic *Protection*. Similarly, while "abundance" isn't on the list, determine to what area of your life you wish to apply that energy. If you desire an abundance of blessings or friends, then *Blessing* or *Friendship* are the topics under which to look, respectively.

Now, just dive in—and enjoy!

Adaptation *(Versatility)*

The art of living does not consist in preserving and clinging to a particular mode of happiness, but in allowing happiness to change its form without being disappointed by the change; happiness, like a child, must be allowed to grow up. —CHARLES L. MORGAN

Life is change, and change is what we make of it. When I first became involved in magick, I was told that this Path was one that was forever transforming. Anything else would mean stagnation and the eventual death of that special spark—that flame within that makes each person (and each person's Art) truly unique and *alive*.

The problem for most practitioners, however, isn't the lack of desire to adapt but the pace at which things are changing in modern times. Computers provide a great example. Most software is already outdated when it first hits the store shelves. Now put our spirituality into that construct—where technology and science are constantly revealing new things about our world and even the Universe. It leaves me out of breath just thinking about it, and I suspect I'm not alone.

So how exactly does a spiritual seeker keep up with the changes in society, knowledge, and even those within himself or herself? The first answer to this question is awareness. If we awaken ourselves and learn to be more aware of those little things that slowly build up toward internal and external evolution, we're much less surprised when the final manifestation happens. No longer will we be caught off guard or left like a spiritual wallflower.

By definition, awareness means being on the ready and living in the moment. It also means staying alert to the patterns that came before, and those just about to emerge. However, awareness only happens when we welcome it into our daily routine. You can accomplish this through a miniritual first thing in the morning.

Morning Awareness Miniritual and Amulet

Get up a little earlier than you normally do each day (it doesn't take long). Have one yellow candle (for the conscious self) and one purple candle (for the spiritual self) on your altar or a handy table. Also have a small token (portable) that represents awareness to you (I like a small magnifying glass for "close looking"). That item should be set between the two candles. Each morning light the yellow candle, then the purple from the yellow, saying:

> *Awaken my mind, open my eyes,*
> *Honor the past, and illuminate where the future lies*
> *In this moment, throughout this day*
> *Keep me aware in every way*
> *I welcome the Spirit of truth*
> *I welcome the Spirit of insight*
> *I welcome the Spirit of versatility and transformation*
> *So mote it be*

Now pick up the item that you've chosen and hold it between the two candles to absorb their light. Repeat the incantation several more times until you feel that item getting warm. This saturates the token with both conscious and logical energy and spiritual sensitivity.

Blow out the candles and carry the token with you where you can hold or touch it periodically, imparting the alert energy you've placed therein. By the way, a cat's-eye or an eye agate are both good choices if you'd prefer to carry a crystal.

Having given you a good way to help your personal changes along, I would also balance that idea by saying there are some things that should *not* change. As Victor Hugo said, *Change your opinions, keep to your principles; change your leaves, keep intact your roots.* I think it's important in the midst of fast and furious transformations to know where our roots lie, and to which ones you need to hold firm. With that in mind, I would offer this idea for a portable amulet that protects those roots, while letting your leaves turn and bend with the wind.

Transformation Amulet

To make this amulet you'll need a leaf from a flower-bearing plant, a root, and a small pouch in which to house them. You need to put the leaf in the pouch by daylight (above ground), and the root by nightfall (below ground). As you put the component parts in say:

> *As above, so below*
> *Let me grow*
> *And keep me whole!*

Repeat this invocation three times (once each for body, mind, and spirit) then carry it with you during times of extreme change.

Air

A great wind is blowing, and that gives you either imagination or a
headache.   —CATHERINE THE GREAT

We will talk briefly about the elements later in this book, but
Granny wants to take a moment to give you ideas on blending Air energy (specifically wind) into your various magickal modalities. See, the
beauty of wind is that it has defined direction. The area from which
each wind flows, and where it moves toward, both have great symbolic
significance.

I have heard numerous writers on the origin point of the winds and
associated symbolic correspondences. Most, however, fail to discuss
how the movement from that origin point through various atmospheric
conditions will inevitably affect the overall character of that wind. We
need to ponder that transformation before applying that energy to our
spells and rituals. Why? Just consider a tiny wind that gets all riled up
and becomes a tornado—the personality difference and spiritual signature is vastly different (and not in a positive way)!

To put this idea into a functional example, the eastern originating
wind is associated with inceptions, the mind, and communication. If
the wind turns toward the North, it then begins moving into earth energy, providing foundations and growth. To me, this makes such a wind
ideal for written or verbal discussions that need an even ground on
which to begin.

Here's a brief chart to give you more ideas along these lines:

ORIGIN	COMPLETION	ENERGY
North	East	strong foundations for a new project
North	South	gently growing passion
North	West	nurturing
West	South	increased emotional energy

ORIGIN	COMPLETION	ENERGY
West	East	effective communication in relationships
West	North	thinking clearly in an emotional situation
South	East	powerful interaction
South	West	intense physicality
South	North	supporting intimate relationships
East	South	mental clarity and energy
East	West	balance head and hearing

This is a very generalized list to which I encourage you to bring your insight for best results.

Alertness

Being alert and aware are two qualities that not only motivate and guide an effective spiritual Path, but every portion of life. In Eastern traditions, an alert approach to life is considered being mindful. From this perspective awareness not *just* about perspectives, it's about everything we accept as truth, about those things with which we fill our thoughts, about what we cling to ... and what we release.

I think it's important to consider the breadth of how awareness affects our actions and reactions. The more aware we become, the less likely we are to be caught off guard, and the more likely we are to catch those whispers from Spirit. The more mindful we are, the more our inner and outer lives reflect that pause to consider the ramifications of each moment. I realize that sounds pretty big, somewhat complex, but it's not easy to describe, simply because each person's alertness and mindfulness is also colored by life's experiences, culture, and society.

Moving into the spiritual arena, our alertness signals the presence of various powers, energies, and their movements. I think it's easy to see why this is a key to effective magickal workings, be they solitary or with a group. Here's one activity you may find helpful to honing this attribute.

Alertness Exercise

Awareness is something that you can improve through practice. If you think of it like a spiritual muscle, the more you exercise your perceptive abilities, the more honed they become. The simplest approach to this is also very pragmatic. Identify a few situations, people, or items about which you'd like to have more awareness. Then pick out one from this list with which to start practicing.

Move yourself to where you can quietly observe that situation, person, or object from a variety of positions (right, left, above, below). As you stop at each point, consider how your perspective changes. Ask yourself questions like:

- What am I seeing now that I did not before?

- How has my sensual input changed?

- How does this new vantage point change my emotional or mental response?

- Has this alternative position provided more information that I need to consider?

- Psychically, do I notice any difference in the energies, or sense something I did not before?

In particular I like to use a large faceted crystal with students when introducing this activity. First I have the student hold the crystal without looking at it closely and write down any feelings they get (if, for example, they feel it would be good for healing or balance). Next I have them examine each facet of the crystal separately.

Each side of a crystal can have unique characteristics. One may have small inclusions, another a slight color change, and another still a phantom. Each of these tiny changes has a different mental and spiritual impact. I have the student write down everything they see, feel, and sense at each side. Finally I have them meditate with their hands cupping the whole crystal again (which is the sum of all its parts) to see if their initial assessment stays the same or changes to reflect the new information they have gathered.

Typically the overall assessment becomes much more detailed. Better still, the way in which the student applies that token becomes much more successful and focused because they have gotten to know the crystal. They took the time to improve awareness in a very determined, direct way. Try it!

Amulets, Charms, Fetishes, and Talismans

Courage and perseverance have a magic talisman, before which difficulties and obstacles vanish into air.　　　　　—JOHN ADAMS

The modern neo-Pagan often uses the terms *amulet, charm, fetish,* and *talisman* interchangeably, even though they are vastly different items with traditionally different applications. The original meanings of these tokens help explain the mixup. Let's begin with charms.

I believe that charms were the first form of portable magick, being comprised of nothing more than words in poetic form (charm comes from a Latin term meaning "song"). While sometimes an object was added to this process (like we see with charm bracelets), ultimately the power of the charm was in the written or spoken word. Key applications for charms included invoking fortune, inspiring love, improving luck, and so forth.

Luck-Invoking Charm

> *Words and wishes to the winds, by my will this spell begins*
> *Luck be quick, Fate be kind, help me in some luck to find*

Amulets, by comparison, have a protective nature. Nonetheless, the Latin term *amuletum* means "a charm." With this in mind it's no wonder the terms get confused! Typically amulets had a physical component (metal, stone, plants) to which the practitioner added a *charm*. This was done during auspicious moon signs, hours, and days to improve the overall power and longevity of the item. An amulet's power remains neutral until called into play by circumstances. This gives the amulet greater longevity.

Travel Amulet

One of the best travel amulets is a small piece of turquoise that's been blessed by a waning moon (so any trouble fades) with an incantation like:

> *As safely in my hands this stone I hold*
> *Keep me safe upon the road*
> *Whether I travel near or far*
> *Spirit protect my little car*

Keep the stone in your glove compartment or on your person if you're biking. Note that you can (and should) change the incantation if you're traveling by air or train.

* * *

Fetishes have some similarity to both charms and amulets. The term seems to have Portuguese roots meaning "to contrive by charm." Sound familiar? As with amulets, these items are made during specific astrological phases out of natural items that evoke a strong emotional or spiritual response in the bearer. That's why you often hear of animal bones or skins being utilized in a fetish because tribal people had strong connections to the spirits represented by those items. For our purposes, small images of a patron god or goddess might be apt.

Cat Kinship Fetish

This is a wonderful little fetish for those of you with beloved cat familiars. For it you'll need a small pouch with pieces of dried catnip, either a whisker or tuft of fur from your cat, and a miniature image of Bast, the Egyptian cat goddess. Note that this image can be from a magazine, a drawing, or a small carving. Tie these together in the pouch saying:

> *Bast,*
> *Cat goddess of joy and revelry*
> *Hear my words, my earnest plea*
> *Bless my _____ with good health*
> *Protect him/her with extra stealth*
> *And as to my heart I hold this tight*
> *Keep him/her healthy with all your might.*
> *So mote it be.*

Fill in the blank with your cat's name, and when you say "hold this tight," hold the fetish to your heart. Keep this fetish with you or on your altar as often as possible.

Finally we come to talismans (a word that means both a preservative amulet or a magickal figure). Where the power of amulets stays latent until needed, the talisman is constantly active. Historically a talisman might have an indwelling spirit captured within, and one that may not be all that happy with the situation. That made working with these items very difficult. These days talismans have predominantly reverted to items on which a specific seal or sign is placed (like a rune) and then empowered by...you guessed it, a charm!

Why go through this song and dance over charms? Because I feel it's very important to understand the differences in the processes behind the applications for each item. Magickal arts, like any other art form, require ongoing refinement and study to reach a level of expertise. In part, this means correcting some of our errors in terminology and resulting methodology. While magick is a highly personal, vision-driving method, we can still honor our roots. That doesn't mean you can't sprinkle in personalization, but I do think it's important from a scholarly position to know whereof we speak.

Anger

Anger kills both laughter and joy. What greater foe is there than anger?
—Tiruvalluvar, fifth-century poet

Legend tells us that Triuvalluvar was a Jain monk or a Hindu outcast priest. In either case, the wisdom of his words is not lost on this seeker. According to studies, domestic abuse, road rage, workplace violence, divorce, and addiction are just a few examples of what can happen when anger is mismanaged or misdirected. It's normal human behavior to get upset from time to time, and even to have a verbal sparring match. The problem starts when the feelings involved in those conflicts seem to find no resolution—meaning that one or more parties don't feel validated or that they haven't gained any ground in terms of understanding by the exchange.

A wise witch knows unresolved anger is harmful to your health, not to mention your pride. When you lose control, you also lose power, and often a whole lot of "face" (as Asians call it). Why let the other guy or gal get the best of you? Instead, let's learn how to control our anger before it controls us. There are several basic things I recommend applying:

1. *A healthy dose of logic.* Since anger is emotional, the rational energy helps balance it out. Specifically, balance your expectations against what is realistically possible considering circumstances.

2. *Problem-solving skills and communication.* If you're not working through the options and communicating effectively, you'll only get more frustrated.

3. *A goodly portion of humor* (which happens to be good soul food).

4. *Environmental changes.* Be they temporary or permanent, cleaning, moving furniture, and other activities that help you get out of a negative space and into a positive one are *good* things.

5. *Exercise or other physical activity.* Walk it out, run, go to the gym or whatever. Use up a little excess energy so you can think clearly.

Metaphysically, to my thinking, the best ally we have in managing anger is meditation. By stopping to meditate, you can quell the negativity, convert it, and redirect it. During the meditative process you'll turn the negative into a positive, then take that energy with you when you go to correct things. This last part—the action—is very important. If your anger and response never gets outward expression, the combination can become a very destructive force. Here are two sample meditations for you to try:

Calming Anger Meditation 1

Begin by getting comfortable. Close your eyes and just breathe. Take three cleansing breaths, slow and steady, in through your nose and out through your mouth. Allow your tension to be carried away with each exhale. Slow the pace of your breathing until one breath connects to the next like a circle of air, and you find yourself feeling far more peaceful.

Know that you are in a safe place. There is no one here to judge you; no one to say what is right or wrong. It's just you and Spirit. This safety allows you to explore your feelings similarly to watching a movie—you can disconnect and simply observe. On your mental landscape, allow the memory of what made your anger come into focus. This time you are just an observer, not a participant. As you watch, what was the first thing that brought forward a physical reaction (like stiffening up or your breathing losing its pace)? This point in the memory is important, it created the spark of your anger.

Once you've identified this you can consider why that moment set you off. Did you feel attacked in some way? Fearful? Confused? Whatever that emotion, identify it and make a mental note of it. In the future you'll be able to recognize similar situations that could leave you feeling out of control by so doing.

Release that emotion with your breathing. Let it go and look at the larger picture. What can you learn from this situation? What actions might you want to take to heal it outwardly and inwardly? Give yourself this gift—release the anger and claim renewal. As you do, allow yourself to become more aware of your body and surroundings once more. Hold tightly to the peace and balance you've just established, and then take action on healing the situation that brought you to this point.

Calming Meditation 2

This meditation is similar to the first but the visualization changes. As you begin your breathing exercise, see a pure white light pouring down from above you. Breathe in this light as if it were air. Let it gather into each molecule of your stress, anger, worry and fear, then release this as darkish red light when you exhale. Continue repeating this process, giving the negative energy to the white light. until the light you take in and that which you exhale are the same, clean, pure hue. When you're at last calm and able to think clearly, consider your next best action and take this peacefulness with you as you head out to do just that.

Again I must stress that anger must, in some form, have expression or it will eat at you as sure as a cancer. It is also a very negative emotion to take with you into magickal workings because it can cause your energy to go very, very awry. While this meditation doesn't work for everyone, it does seem to help in combination with the basic efforts suggested previously.

Animals

Man, of all the animals, is probably the only one to regard himself as a great delicacy.
—JACQUES COUSTEAU

Nearly all neo-Pagans I know have a soft spot for animals: dogs, cats, lizards, birds, fish, ferrets, whatever! This, at least in part, is connected to our love of nature and its inhabitants. It also has to do with the longstanding symbolic value of those inhabitants, and their place in various spiritual practices.

While I could share with you dozens of ancient approaches to what I call "wild" magick, I think that perhaps modern neo-Pagans need to consider animals in a different way. Since many of us live in areas devoid of natural viewing, and many of us live in apartments where pets are not allowed, we're dealing with a whole new set of circumstances. It's unlikely, for example, for anyone to run into a moose in an urban environment (unless you happen to live in Alaska!). However, it may not be so unlikely to see images of moose on various items—like a match cover, a painting, a T-shirt, and so forth.

It is this aspect of animal energy that I'd like to discuss in this book because I think it's one that has (for the most part) been overlooked. Most people who have practiced magick for even a short number of years know basic animal omens and signs. They may also know various charms and spells for their animal companions. But, what most of us have not considered is animal symbolism as it directly impacts our daily life even in the concrete jungle, not to mention how to apply that symbolic energy effectively.

Returning to the example of a moose, say images of this creature keep appearing everywhere you go. You see one on TV, glimpse one on a bumper sticker, or see one on a restaurant marquee. This seems to be a pretty good indication that the moose spirit is trying to get your attention. But what, pray tell, is moose saying?

Well let's start with basic representative value. Native Americans consider moose as the guardian of the North, the region of wisdom. Moose tries to teach us the balance between gentleness and strength in both word and deed. It also speaks loudly of self-esteem. So, consider where you saw these images or heard the word *moose*. If all the incidents were verbal, then I'd say you need to consider how others perceive your communications. If you saw the images only when going to work, then maybe the way you're handling your job needs reassessment. See how that works?

If you're looking for good references on animal symbolism, I'd recommend reading *Animal Spirit* (by myself and Rowan Hall) combined with the book *Symbolic and Mythological Animals* by J. C. Cooper. Cooper's book provides you with a plethora of global interpretations to ponder, while *Animal Spirit* looks at spiritual applications and provides examples from which to work.

Now, I expect some of you are wondering...okay, besides understanding when an animal spirit is speaking, how else can this symbolism be applied? Well, if you read older collections of magick you'll notice animal parts are often prescribed for spells. That's because people trusted in the animal spirit's power. Since we don't wish to misuse nature, we can use replacements—magazine pictures, small carvings, or drawings instead of the animal. As long as we remember that in sacred spaces an object is every bit as powerful as what it represents, and honor that power, it will work just as effectively.

Potential Replacements for Animal Parts and Symbolism

- Small carvings or figurines (these are often found at gift shops in a variety of media from glass and porcelain to stone)

- Metal charms (like for bracelets)

- Photographs or paintings

- Pictures from books or magazines (like *National Geographic*)

- Wood carvings

- Product labels, logos, business cards

- Beads (bead stores often have a wide variety of animal images)

- Buttons, bumper stickers

- Toys and games (like Monopoly figures or plastic barn animals)

- Found animal parts (caution: these may carry disease!)

To provide some examples, a South American spell calls for the use of an alligator tooth for luck and protection. Now, none of us are going to go wrestle an alligator for a tooth. We could, however, use the image of an alligator, perhaps a child's toy, as the component for a spell that protects good fortune. Or, in Europe, a chameleon's tongue was used for legal success as well as a love charm. Combine those two, and the image of a chameleon might be ideal for relationship-oriented legal issues.

In any case, the key to success is that the symbolism makes sense to you. Without that emotional and spiritual connection, you'll be spinning your wheels. While I obviously think it's valuable to learn animal correspondences, that's only really the beginning of our knowledge. To this foundation we should add some serious thought. Meditate on the histocultural meanings and ask yourself how those values influence our current perspectives, how they've changed, and how our personal feelings toward that creature should influence its symbolic applications in our magick. This blend creates a powerful alliance between history and vision that improves the success of your efforts.

Apathy

Strive for passion, lest all else wither away.

—ITALIAN POEM, C. 1400

I worry greatly over the apathy I see in the world today—the feeling that one person can't make a difference. This numbness leads to complacency, where little things that could be vital to our future pass us by without notice. Interestingly enough, in the early stages of the Church, the term *apathy* expressed contempt toward earthly concerns. But witches, being tied to the earth as a classroom and its inhabitants, shouldn't fall prey to this null zone. Be it societal, political, economic, educational, or spiritual—apathy is dangerous to our way of life and acts like a dampening field on our magick.

It's normal, however, for everyone to experience those moments when energy drops, discouragement sets in, and you just don't want to keep trying. When those times come, you have two choices: give in to the feeling or get up and do something constructive. Very often, the action helps shift your mood, but when you need a little more of a boost, here are a couple of activities to try:

Banish the Blues

For this spell you'll need a blue candle and a white candle. At dawn (the time of renewed hope), light the blue candle saying:

> *Let negativity return from whence it came*
> *I give my apathy to this flame*
> *Burn away, burn away*
> *With the dawning of the day*

Light the white candle from the blue one then blow out the blue one saying:

> *I have stolen your fire*
> *Negativity has no power over me*
> *I give myself to light, to hope and to action*
> *This is the flame of motivation*
> *It burns within me. So mote it be.*

I suggest destroying the blue candle (break it up to break up the negative energy you put inside). Keep the white candle and light it any time you feel your resolve waning.

Apathy Amulet

This is a nice portable token that helps stave off apathy and its negative effects. Take a yellow cloth or pouch (the cloth needs to be big enough to bundle sachet-style). Place a tiger's-eye (for the sun's bless-ings and motivation), a pinch of saffron, some sage, and sandalwood powder inside). Bless this by saying something like:

> *With the power of the sun, and by my will—this spell's begun*
> *Saffron and sage motivate*
> *Sandalwood—negativity abates!*
> *All within this cloth of gold*
> *By my will this spell unfolds!*

When you feel you need a change in perspectives quickly, take a little of the herbal mixture out of the pouch and release it to the winds, reciting the same incantation but change the line "all within this cloth of gold" to "released from within this cloth of gold." Refill the pouch as soon as possible.

By the way, I think that very often we can avoid the apathy trap just by remaining aware and alert. For help along those lines, return to the be-ginning of this chapter!

Aromatherapy

If the day and the night are such that you greet them with joy, and life emits a fragrance like flowers and sweet-scented herbs, is more elastic, more starry, more immortal—that is your success. All nature is your congratulation... —HENRY DAVID THOREAU

The art of aromatherapy originated several thousand years ago. We see evidence that the Egyptians, Hebrews, Greeks, and Babylonians alike used aromatics not only for healing but also in religious settings. Nonetheless, the actual term *aromatherapy* is only about fifty years old, having been coined by a French chemist named Maurice Gottefosse. It is from Gottefosse's work that we gain most of our contemporary insights into this art.

It seems that our ancestors were utilizing the subtle psychological and physiological effects of various scents. Think of your mother's perfume. How does that memory make you feel? Or think of the incredible aroma of your favorite food cooking. Does your tummy rumble? These are exactly the kinds of reactions that give aromatherapy its power. Now all you're going to do is apply the idea metaphysically.

Here is a list of various aromatic herbs and their traditional correspondences for magick.

SCENT	CORRESPONDENCE
Apple	Joy
Cedar	Courage
Cinnamon	Luck
Geranium	Bravery, safety
Jasmine	Gentle love, meditative focus
Lavender	Sleep, rest, tranquility
Lilac	Peace, conscious mind
Mint	Prosperity

SCENT	CORRESPONDENCE
Myrrh	Protection (banishing), purification
Sandalwood	Spirituality, Psychism
Vanilla	Passion, Power
Vervain	Fertility
Violet	Well-being

Using this list isn't difficult. Just get creative. Dab an aromatic oil on your household light fixtures and literally light up the energy each time you turn them on. Toss aromatic herbs tied into a sock in your dryer and charge your wardrobe. Pick meaningful flowers and let their scent and beauty communicate without words. Make magickal potpourri, and of course, if you're a kitchen witch like Granny, you'll cook with them, too, so everyone internalizes that wonderful, warm sentiment.

The beauty of aromatherapy is its subtlety. No one thinks twice about a gentle scent passing by. They might stop to admire it, but humans don't overanalyze it. Thus it works on a subconscious level, which is also tied into how well magick manifests. Without that connection, the results decrease. So you can use aromas to support your goals on all levels of BE-ing.

Aura

Why not walk in the aura of magic that gives the small things of life their uniqueness and importance? Why not befriend a toad today?

—Germaine Greer

Modern metaphysics descrbes the aura as a field of energy that surrounds all living things. The condition of this field reveals much about the condition of life within. Think of this like a spiritual atmosphere. The proverbial weather pattern of your aura illustrates how stormy or calm you are in body, mind, and spirit. Thus learning to sense this sphere and becoming aware when it shifts or changes is also an important part of knowing the self better. In turn that awareness cues you as to what type of magick, if any, you can effectively enact at any given moment.

A minority of people are fortunate enough to be able to see auras. For most of the rest of us, when we begin to extend our senses to become more aware of auric energies, our minds will interpret that energy through the sense to which we relate most strongly. So, you might come to discover that auras communicate to you through smell, textural cues, tastes, and sounds. I mention this so you don't anticipate one thing and miss good sensual cues in the process.

So, exactly how do you interpret these sensual cues? Here's a list to get you started:

SMELL, TASTE, OR TEXTURE	MEANING
Itchy	Discomfort or dishonesty
Hard	Protective (not open), a loner
Soft	Gentility and compassion
Jagged	Anger or tension
Sticky	Clingy personality, not releasing the past
Bulge or bump	Possible area of injury or disease
Loud sounds	Boisterous personality, high energy
Melodic sounds	Peaceful and balanced
Static	Communication problems
Overly sweet	Putting on airs
Bitter aroma	Tension, blockage, sarcastic or bitter personality
Forest aroma	Improved strength or outlooks
Spicy	Adventurous, enthusiastic

These are generalizations at best, but you get the idea. Always begin your adventure in auras with yourself. As you find the best way to sense your own, and make note of it, also make note of your physical, mental, and emotional conditions at that time. This will provide you with an even better guide as to what your aura is trying to tell you. When you get really good at this awareness personally, you can then extend it to your interactions with others. Just be careful that you don't overstep personal boundaries in this exploration. The aura is very personal. If you're trying to understand someone better and want to get close enough to really interact with his or her aura, it's polite to ask first.

Balance

When you cannot make up your mind between two evenly balanced courses of action, choose the bolder. —WILLIAM JOSEPH SLIM

The balance between everyday life and spiritual, between head and heart, between the temporal and eternal—this is like a waltz that humankind has been trying to learn. And while the struggle between head and heart has been around for a long time, the spiritual disconnection has not. In particular, modern people seem to have fallen into an odd spiritual compartmentalization that seems to have developed side by side with technology in the last hundred years or so. Rather than blend spirituality with the 9 to 5 world, it got put on a shelf and dusted off once a week or once a year as needed.

Thankfully it seems that the New Age thrust to bring spiritual matters back into focus is also helping to offset this trend. Most magickal practitioners already know the importance of living and BE-ing the magick, but actually getting to that point is a whole other matter. Unfortunately, most of us aren't ready to ascend just yet, so we're still working on this point! The question is, then, how do we begin to re-establish symmetry?

I think the first step is identifying the areas of your life that are most out of whack, and there are a lot of potential combinations here, including:

Mind—Body	Self—Others
Mind—Spirit	Self—World
Body—Spirit	Self—Spirit
Spirituality—Daily life	Work—Play
Needs—Wants	Logic—Instinct

Once you identify the key areas where balance should be applied in healthier doses, then you can go about constructing both mundane and metaphysical methods for correcting the situation.

For example, say you have been feeling disconnected spiritually. You've been physically active and mentally alert, but that third part of the equation seems to be missing. In this case, I'd say that meditation and some type of spellcraft or miniritual might be a good solution. You have all the concrete stuff already in place (mind/body) but spirit is more elusive. It's like playing tag with the wind, and it also relies heavily on faith.

Body-Mind Spirit Equilibrium Visualization

For this meditation it's best to sit up straight in a semilotus position so your body forms a triangle (your head being the top of the triangle). This shape stresses the threefold nature. I also suggest waiting until a day when you're well rested and feeling fairly relaxed. Stress and weariness affect the results of this activity negatively.

As you sit, visualize your body as it is, but not in a physical sense. Rather let your mind and senses become aware of your auric envelope. You can still hear your heartbeat, and the comforting rhythm of your breath, but it's part of this shell of light energy. Now, realize that thought is a type of energy too. As you watch yourself in this mental gallery, notice how little flashes of light leave your mind and dance throughout the aura, giving your body signals.

Next, consider that you have the ability to control those signals. Take a moment and send one from your third eye to your right knee. Now continue that cycle and let the same flicker move to your left knee, then back up to your head to create a full, light circle. Repeat this process, sending out a steady stream of light energy until your body, mind, and spirit all connect continuously in that cycle. Stay like this as long as you wish, then return to normal awareness and make notes of your experiences. Specifically, how did your perceptions and sensations change during the meditation? How do you feel now? More connected and centered? If so, you enacted the activity correctly!

By the way, meditation can help with several issues of connection. It improves one's awareness of the mind, mind-body, and mind-body-spirit relationship. It can help us analyze our needs versus our wants from an emotional distance. It can release the inner child, or the inner God/dess as required by a situation. If you'd like to explore meditation further, please read the section under that heading later in this book, which goes into far more detail about methods and goals, including adding visualizations to the process.

Mind you, I would not recommend using meditation as your only avenue for achieving balance (that, in itself, would be unbalanced). Rather I would suggest blending the most successful metaphysical methods with other mundane efforts. This keeps you active and involved with your life and path on all levels.

Banishing

Confront the dark parts of yourself, and work to banish them with illumination and forgiveness. Your willingness to wrestle with your demons will cause your angels to sing. Use the pain as fuel, as a reminder of your strength.
—AUGUST WILSON

There are energies and entities in this world that are anything but productive to positive spiritual living. In those times when you feel swal-

lowed by negativity, a streak of bad luck, psychically attacked, or pos-
sessed by bad habits, that's the time to consider a banishing.

The first step in this process is to know from where the problem
comes. You can't get a weed completely out of a garden unless you dig
out the whole root. Similarly, it's very difficult to banish anything if
you're uncertain as to the source. This isn't the kind of energy you want
to apply haphazardly. If you must use a generalized banishing, try to
take precautions so that the energy gets directed for the greatest good.
This allows the Universe to step in and fill out the part of the bigger
picture you cannot see or sense.

I think of banishing as a specific pattern. It's one that takes the energy at hand and turns it. It can go back where it came, it can be directed into the Earth (Mom knows how to handle "dirt"), it can be
dispersed, or it can be transformed. Since we cannot destroy energy
(that is a physical law), I like the last option best because it makes a
positive out of a negative. To accomplish this I use an elemental banishing. Why elemental? Well, since Wiccans call on the four elements to
protect and empower sacred space, it only seems natural to call on them
to turn away unwanted energy too!

Elemental Banishing

For this activity you need a piece of paper, a small plastic container,
a brazier, and some soil (from your yard is fine). On the piece of paper
describe that which you want to banish. Be as specific as possible and
hold an image of that person, energy, or problem firmly in mind as you
write. When you're done cross the whole thing out with a huge X and
crumple it up like you might do with garbage.

Put the crumpled paper in the plastic container and cover it with
water. Freeze this (for one thing this slows or halts the negativity). As you
place it into the back of your freezer invoke the element of water saying:

> Guardian of the West and water
> Hear my request

> *Quell this situation with your healing waves*
> *And take the negativity with you on the tides of transformation*

Leave this in the freezer for one week from the waning to the dark moon.

At sundown on the night of the dark moon, defrost the paper and dry it. As soon as it's dry, ignite it with a match and put it in the brazier while you invoke the element of fire:

> *Guardian of the South and fire*
> *Hear my request*
> *Burn away any remnants of negativity*
> *Replace them with the light of hope*

Let this burn completely to ashes.

When the ashes cool enough, take them outside and release them to the air before you (hold them in your hand and sprinkle them down toward the Earth). Invoke the element of Air saying:

> *Guardian of the East and Air*
> *Hear my request*
> *Disperse the negativity that once was*
> *And release it to the winds of change*

Finally step firmly on the ashes (symbolically taking back the reigns of control and power in this matter). As you do invoke the element of Earth saying:

> *Guardian of the North and Earth*
> *Hear my request*
> *Ashes to ashes, dust to dust*
> *Take what was, turn it into your soils, and let*
> *Something positive grow in its place.*
> *I thank you, the Air, the Fire, and Water for your aid*
> *So mote it be.*

I would issue several words of caution on this process. First, be careful how you word a banishing. I'd personalize the above process so it better reflects the specific situation by its wording. Why? Well, I know one young lady who sought to rid her office of bad vibes and ended up banishing all her coworkers! Second, if you're going to banish a bad habit, you'd better be ready to work on that aspect of self honestly. All your magick will do little good (if any) otherwise. Third, if you're banishing a person as a means of protection, take care that such does not harm that individual in any way. Generally speaking I've found this process very successful when I follow that guideline.

Beauty

Beauty can be feasted upon.   —CHINESE PROVERB

The wise and insightful witch believes in the old saying that beauty is born within. The media and society often put a lot of stock in outward appearances, but in spiritual pursuits the inner person is far more important. While it's normal to be influenced by our culture's concept of beauty, the care and feeding of the Sacred Self demands that we have a broader perspective of what that word really means.

Plato found beauty in simplicity. Pythagoras felt that form and structure created a foundation of loveliness (rather like a dynamic fingerprint). Pliny the Elder felt that there was much more to beauty than met the eye—that everything from carriage to intellect modified the way we perceive others, and ourselves, and Greek philosophy discussed beauty as something that defied all natural laws. These very esoteric terms from ancient minds give me pause to wonder what happened to that kind of depth in human consciousness. Truly the modern idea of beauty is rather superficial and shallow.

Having said that, there are times when everyone wants to feel and look his or her best. And I see no reason why we cannot gather up a bit of the inner beauty we've achieved and express it outwardly using tried-'n'-true magickal methods. From applying May Day dew to our face to a glamorous glamoury, there have been hundreds of spells and potions put forward through the ages to help us in our quest.

The one approach I'd like to discuss here begins with the phrase "Thou art God/dess." This witch believes that a spark of the Divine resides within each one of us. If we let that spark shine out to the world, the natural beauty that goes with it will also shine. This is not an intense, knock-your-socks-off presentation, but a warm, welcoming fire that invites everyone to its side. Rather than put people off because of too much flash and fanfare, the idea here is to simply be the best of who and what you are, and wholly comfortable in your skin.

Inner Beauty Visualization

Now as someone who has often *not* been comfortable with Self, my way of working on this issue is using bath and shower time for meditations and visualizations. Specifically, set up candles, incense, special music, aromatics—anything you can think of that makes you feel special and pampered (honest, you deserve it). Then as you soak in the tub or stand in the shower imagine that the water is the white-silvery light of Spirit's blessings. Let this light fill you from inside out, specifically your aura, to the point of saturation (you'll actually feel as if your skin is glowing).

When you're done, get out and look at yourself in the mirror. If you let your vision blur slightly you should see that divine glow on the edges of your awareness. Take that energy with you into any day where you need a little extra boost. Generally I find the overall effect lasts at least twenty-four hours.

Dress for Success

Another way to charge your aura with whatever magick you need on any particular day is by combining aromatics with your clothing. To accomplish this simply toss a cloth with essential oil into your dryer with your outfit for that day (or a bundle of dry herbs). This charges your entire wardrobe! Some potential aromatics include:

- Catnip—overall beauty and playfulness
- Thyme—self assurance
- Lavender—happiness and harmony
- Violet—luck
- Lily—mental awareness
- Ginger—energy boost
- Bay—psychic sensitivity
- Peach—wisdom

Remember to keep your goals in mind as you dress (i.e., "put on" the magick). Imagine yourself in whatever setting to which you're going being fully "on"—confident, attractive, and successful.

Blessing

Just to be is a blessing. Just to live is holy.
—Rabbi Abraham Heschel

We use the phrase *blessed be* frequently but I often wonder if we truly understand what we're saying. First, it's an interesting historical fact that the word bless is taken from a root word meaning blood. This dates back to the times when altars were prepared for the Divine by sprinkling blood over the surface. While at first this sounds a little gruesome, we must remember that blood represents life's essence.

Going further, *bless* also means to set apart, protect, make happy, liberation from temporal concerns, and consecration. Putting this together with the original linguistics, when we say *"blessed be"* we are invoking all the best things in life, including safety, joy, and enlightenment, on one another. That's quite a mouthful!

Now let's take this to a more personal level. What about blessing our loved ones, our pets, our homes, and ourselves? Aren't these people and places worthy of "blessed bes"? My answer is a definitive *yes*, but sometimes I think we neglect to turn the function of blessing back to hearth and home. This happens in part because many folks are still a little nervous about the idea of being a Priest/ess in their own lives. It also happens because we seem to equate "self blessing" with "selfishness," which is simply not true. Consider: How can we hope to bless others effectively when we don't know how to receive blessings in our own lives?

House Blessing

Native Americans often use sage and sweetgrass or lavender along with a prayer feather to bless a home. If you live in an urban environment you might want to do this at least once a month to deter cumulative stray energies from lodging in the walls. Or, do it weekly as part of your regular cleaning "ritual."

Start in the main room of the house (perhaps the kitchen) and move clockwise through the home. As you enter a new room, wave the smoke around saying: *Let all who enter here be blessed.* If you have a specific household God or Goddess, invoke the deities by name (and perhaps light a white candle in each room to represent Spirit's presence).

When you're finished, douse the sage wand in water and put it neatly away for future use (store it on your altar or another safe spot).

Pet Blessing

Since animals get nervous around burning items, I suggest making a charm for your pet that you regularly charge with "blessed be" energies. Good options include a reflective nametag or a bell that easily attaches to the creature's collar. Energize this token in sunlight (a symbol of blessing) while holding your hand down over it thinking of how much your pet means to you. Let that loving, warm energy flow out of your hands into the token.

To this process you can add a prayer or incantation like:

> *Lord of the Animals, Lady of the Land keep* _____ *safe and healthy*
> *Saturate this token with all good things so that wherever* _____ *roams*
> *They are protected and happy*
> *So be it.*

If your animal is an indoor pet, you may not have to recharge this very often (typically the dangers in a house are less than outside). For wandering pets I encourage monthly recharging (perhaps when you bless your house!).

And what about yourself? How about enacting some type of blessing ritual or spell on your birthday every year? On this day you celebrate your soul's arrival on this earth. Why not commemorate it by bringing some "good stuff" your way? Wiccans often accomplish this by dabbing personally preferred anointing oil on the various chakras while speaking an affirmation. One example would be dabbing some on the soles of your feet saying *"I walk the Path of beauty with confidence"* or if you'd like to invite the Divine into this, *"Goddess bless my Path with confidence."* Continue with the other chakras and blessings as you feel inspired.

Body Art

One must be a work of art, or wear a work of art.

—OSCAR WILDE

For roughly 30,000 years, men and women alike have used tattoos to enhance and modify their skin. Egyptian mummies dating to 4200 B.C.E. bear tattoos, and the oldest known remains of a tattooed body comes to us from a glacier in Italy and date to the Bronze Age (5,000 years ago). This man's arms, torso, and legs were adorned with images of various mythical creatures.

It would seem that the art of tattooing evolved alongside humankind's awareness of self, society, and spirituality. In some cultures tattoos were a visual history (for Tahitians in particular). For others they were a personal expression of uniqueness, a brand of station (Rome), a way to commemorate unusual experiences (sailors) or a way to honor various social and cultural traditions. Of the three, this last application was by far the most historically prevalent. Why? Because humans are tribal creatures, and the tattoo could express a sense of belonging and connection to that all-important unit.

Incidentally, the word *tattoo* is thought to originate in either Polynesia or Tahiti from the root *tatau*, which simply means "to mark." Body art practices spanned the globe and continue in popularity today, especially among the neo-Pagan subculture. After having been outlawed or suppressed, it's estimated that some 40 million people in North America alone have one or more tattoos.

For many people a tattoo still represents one way to reconnect with something or someone, and make that connection permanent (as opposed to so many things in life which seem fleeting). Other people use it as a way to mark notable transitions in their lives, or things toward which they feel passionate and committed. Others still just enjoy the ornamentation akin to wearing earrings or a bracelet (that you can never lose!). The reasons are as personalized as the individual, but we do seem to be reaching out for some type of tribal experience, and it's one that also binds people with tattoos together. Just simple observation of human nature indicates that the more commonalities people have, the more likely they are to communicate. Tattoos open the door for that initial communication as a touchstone of sorts.

If you're considering a tattoo, it's good to think long and hard about what you want, and why you want it. A tattoo artist once told me to pick out an image then wait a year (thank you, Dino!). As it happened I waited four, but it was still the best advice I ever got. When the time is right, and the pattern right—the tattoo feels as if it's always been there. Be forewarned that people rarely get just one tattoo. Once you've gone through this experience you find yourself thinking of your whole body as a potential canvas waiting for expression!

For those who might like a "test run" to be certain, the option of henna tattoos exist. Henna is an herb, and Mehendi, an art of temporary tattooing with henna, originated in India. Mehendi traditionally are applied to the hands or feet for special ceremonies (like marriage) but many women have been applying the idea outside that setting. For example, one woman I know had a henna tattoo just prior to giving birth as a way to welcome the new spirit into the world. The beauty of Mehendi is that it disappears in four weeks and is completely painless. Anyone interested in a tattoo to mark similar special occasions, but who is hesitant to have the tattoo forever, would do well to explore this alternative as documentation indicates that up to 50 percent of those who get tattoos regret them later.

Why the regrets? The answers range from short-sightedness that occurred in a nonpermanent relationship to realizing what they thought was "cute" or "cool" fifteen years ago simply turns out to be neither in maturity. Other reasons included issues with employers, the reaction of family and friends, allergic reactions to the dye, and the inability to donate blood for a year after getting the tattoo. So while tattooing has the capacity to provide a cultural bridge of sorts, it's not without potential negative consequences.

Candle Magick

Bell, book and candle shall not drive me back when gold and silver becks
me to come on.   —WILLIAM SHAKESPEARE

Candle magick is among the oldest and simplest forms of spellcraft.
Because candles were a common household item, it makes perfect sense
that our ancestors would utilize them for spiritual functions. The beautiful light of a candle banished the darkness, and quickly came to represent Spirit and the ongoing quest for enlightenment. This symbolic
value hasn't waned in the least, and it's nearly humorous to think of any
neo-Pagan space that doesn't contain at least one candle.

There are times, however, when we overlook simple, handy magickal
solutions because we live is a society where fancy = better. Nonetheless,
Granny is here to tell you that candles make wonderful tools and focus
points for your Art. Better still, most supermarkets now carry a variety
of colors, shapes, and scents from which the clever Cunning Person
may choose freely without anyone thinking twice about the end use!

Here is a list of creative ways to use candles in your Craft with little fuss:

- Create your own during auspicious astrological times so the
  candle's energy bears your purpose even during the creation
  process.

- Choose your candle's colors according to your goals.

- Anoint the candle with symbolic aromatic oils.

- Carve the candles with symbols of your intention (or find ones of a suitable shape).

- Place the candles on your altar and/or the four quarters, and light them to invite the Powers.

- Use the candle's flame or wax patterns in divination.

- Adorn the area around the candle with items that visually support your goal, then light it each morning while speaking your wish.

- Add candles to your meditation space for ambiance.

- In a group setting have each person bring a candle to the altar to represent their part of the greater whole.

- Light candles as part of daily prayers or affirmations.

- Blow out candles to release magick, or the sacred space.

Remember to light your candles with focus and intention. This is a powerful symbol of reigniting the spiritual fires within and directing them to where you most need that energy to go.

Cartomancy

*Free will and determinism are like a game of cards. The hand that is dealt
you is determinism. The way you play your hand is free will.*
—NORMAN COUSINS

The method of divining the future through cards is technically
called cartomancy. While any ordinary deck of cards can be used for
this, most Witches gravitate to one of the numerous tarot decks created specifically for this purpose. Historians trace the tarot to the
Middle Ages. While it may have come from Egypt by way of the
Gypsies, the most easily documented beginnings appear in Italy
around the fourteenth century. These early cards had but twenty-two
symbols, which later became the Major Arcana. This was later combined with a Chinese version of the tarot, comprised of fifty-six cards
to make what we now easily recognize as the modern seventy-eight-card
deck. By 1540 the first book describing cartomancy appeared and included information on the values for the suit of coins in the tarot.

Now there are literally hundreds of decks from which you can
choose one that really speaks to your higher self. Nonetheless, Granny
suggests you study several decks and compare the values for each card.
This gives you a multidimensional image of what this symbolism means
in a more global setting. For example, I compared the Rider Waite tarot
to the Whimsical tarot for the Magician. These are my notes:

The Magician:

Keynotes: Concentration, Focus, Balance, Inventiveness, Change
The Magician card is numbered one in the Major Arcana,
indicating its importance to the whole. The Rider Waite tarot
depicts the Magician as a man standing with one hand pointing to the sky, the other to the earth—a dramatic portrait of
the "as above, so below" spiritual axiom. Before him are the

tools of his mystical trade—the cup, the sword, the wand, the pentacle (which also happen to correspond to the four suits of the Minor Arcana!). Meanwhile in the Whimsical tarot we have the image of a proud Puss-'n'-boots, acting as the master of ceremonies for the entire deck! The cat appears with all the other traditional symbolism, but brings with him a beloved childhood story to which we can all relate.

When the magician card appears, it traditionally represents creativity, individuality, and transformation. The Magician of Rider Waite's deck can turn any situation around and faces every challenge with a keen wit and know-how. In the case of Puss-'n'-Boots, this cat definitely can land on his or her feet. The lesson here is that by applying creativity to the situation at hand, one is far more likely to land a proverbial fish and some well-deserved cream too!

I think you can see how comparing the two decks gave me a little more food for thought that I can easily apply to a reading. Also, you can take this process a little further by comparing various cards as they might apply to specific areas of your life (work, love, spirituality, travel, etc.). This process not only helps you memorize the cards more easily, but improves your ability to interpret them accurately.

Choices

Destiny is not a matter of chance; it is a matter of choice. It is not a thing to be waited for; it is a thing to be achieved.

—WILLIAM JENNINGS BRYAN

At the outset of this book we discussed adaptation and transformation. On the heels of both comes the ultimate choice(s) we must make. These days choice is usually not simply a crossroad, but a busy intersection among many different potential streets, and several of those streets seem promising. Be it a relationship, jobs, or the route you take to work, the options often seem overwhelming. Can we use magick to help us here?

Granny GoodWitch says yes, but with caution. If you can make a decision using a little research, elbow grease, and thoughtful reflection, that's the way you should go. On the other hand, when the options seem too tempting or too numerous to begin sorting them out mentally, then spiritual approaches can really be of assistance.

First, I'd suggest consulting with your instincts. Is there something inside of you encouraging you to lean in a particular direction? Make note of this gut level feeling on a piece of paper right at the top. All too often when we don't listen to those instincts, we regret it.

Next, consider what might be holding you back. If this "something" can be changed—do so. For example, if you know you'd like to pursue a specific career change but need more training in order to compete, find out how to get that training. Again, this is a great example of times when the rational self comes in handy.

And when push comes to shove, try a little creative divination to help you. I like using a pendulum for guidance in decisions because you can get fairly clear yes-no answers. Here's one example:

Decision Divination

Draw a circle on a white piece of paper. Then draw two intersecting lines on it from North to South and East to West (creating a bull's-eye). Set this on a table and get your pendulum. I prefer something with a defined point so that an oddly weighted object cannot skew the reading; however, some people use rings or herb bundles. Whatever you choose, try to make sure that if it's not a prefabricated pendulum you use something that has symbolic value to your question (rings, for example, pertain to commitments and relationships).

Next, put your elbow firmly on the surface outside the pendulum circle you've drawn. Hold the pendulum so the point is in the center of the bull's-eye. Steady it, then remove your other hand. Finally, begin thinking about the various options before you and ask questions. For example, if this pertains to a job you might ask:

- Will remaining in my present job provide enough income?

- Will staying here make me happy?

- Can I overcome the present difficulties?

- Should I consider a job with _____ (name of firm)?

- Should I consider a career change to _____ (name of job type)?

- Should I develop my transferable skills (transferable skills allow you to take what you've learned in other industries and apply them elsewhere)?

- Is my coworker gossiping against me?

- Will my job be eliminated in the next year?

If the pendulum moves up and down that's an affirmative answer, while left-right movements are a negative reply. Remember to carefully stop the pendulum in between each question you ask so that it's not still moving (the movement is the energy you've created by your question. If you don't stop the pendulum it will be influenced by the previous question).

Chores

*Some people regard discipline as a chore. For me, it is a kind of order that
sets me free to fly.* —JULIE ANDREWS

I have a fondness for the above quote, and for one by Martin Van Buren
that goes: It is easier to do a job right than to explain why you didn't.
These two in tandem perfectly reflect this witch's approach to chores.
For one thing, I'd rather just get them done so I have more time to
relax. For another, I find I'm happier with myself when tasks are done
correctly. Third, I've discovered that when you undertake a chore with a
smile in your heart, the work becomes much easier. However, I must
confess that it's really hard to find that inner grin when scrubbing floors
or doing dishes!

My solution to this has been to find ways to make my chores into
magickal or spiritual practices. When I work on the rugs, for example,
I visualize any sickness or negativity being sucked up by the vacuum
cleaner. In many ways, this turns every chore into what Buddhists call a
moving meditation where the mind focuses on one thing and allows
that concept to settle into your spirit. Here's a list of other potential
applications for various chores:

Magick of the Mundane

- *Laundry:* Add a little aromatic tincture into the wash water to
  saturate your clothes with whatever energy you need. Or, if
  you've been sick, use a purifying scent to get rid of any lingering dis-ease.

- *Lawn mowing:* A great time to meditate and connect with the
  earth through your feet. Grass equates to earth's hair . . . so run
  your toes through it gleefully!

- *Feeding the pets:* I like to sprinkle a spell into my cat's food every morning for health and happiness.

- *Walking the dog:* Moving creates a lot of good energy. As I walk I think of goals that I hope to accomplish and direct that energy into the goal. Or, I use the time to pray or mentally recite positive affirmations.

- *Making dinner:* As a kitchen witch I love putting warm, nurturing energy into food so that everyone internalizes it.

- *Washing windows:* A great analogy to opening yourself to the light of Spirit. Alternatively a good time to commune with the fire (sun) element and water element combined.

- *Weeding the garden:* What weeds need pulling in your spirit and your life? Great symbolic value here—just put it into action. Name your weeds, and pull them neatly out, root and all.

- *Dusting:* When I dust, I concentrate on cleaning away the old, unhealthy habits in my life and starting with a clean slate. Alternatively some ancient civilizations used dust as a divinatory tool. Scan the surface for patterns before wiping those messages away (hmm... wonder what my coffee table is telling me?).

- *Sweeping (broom):* The broom is one of the oldest tools in a witch's kit. Sweep outward to push away negativity, or inward to attract luck into your home. Set a broom near your bed for fertility, dance with it near your garden to encourage the vegetables and flowers to grow high, and shake a wet broom outside to bring rain!

- *Washing walls:* You know that old saying "if walls could talk"? Well, very often they can and do! Walls, like every other part of our house, collect memories. If you've been in a home for only a short time and get the odd feeling that something isn't quite right, use your wall-washing time to connect with the residual memory patterns there. If need be, you're also in an ideal place to pour white light into those patterns to purify and protect.

As you can see, with a little creativity magick translates into mundane life very well, including those things that we don't always enjoy doing. Nonetheless, I have found that bringing the spiritual dimension to bear really helps make the task go by more quickly and with the least amount of displeasure.

Cleansing *(Spiritual Housekeeping)*

There is an electric fire in human nature tending to purify—so that among these human creatures there is continually some birth of new heroism. The pity is that we must wonder at it, as we should at finding a pearl in rubbish. —JOHN KEATS

I love to share a true personal story that illustrates why personal spiritual hygiene is so important. It begins about sixteen years ago when a dear friend started to visit our new home. She came by just to chat on several occasions, and every time after she left I found myself tired and angry for no apparent reason. It took about four visits before I realized that my friend was accidentally dumping all her psychic garbage at my threshold. I hadn't set up my home's wards to filter that out—only to filter out *purposeful* attacks. This was something wholly unconscious on her part, so it walked right through the door and bit me!

Each person *should* ideally be responsible for his or her own spiritual housekeeping. Nonetheless, we do not live in an ideal world, and even some of the most adept practitioners I know are guilty of mismanaging various auric energies. That's where regular cleansing and purification processes become very important. I'm not just talking about your home here, but also work, your car, and your *self!*

People prefer different methods of cleansing and purification, depending on the item or circumstances that require this type of magick. Here are just a few for your consideration:

Cleansing Components

- *Water:* One of the original symbols of purity and cleansing, water is fantastic for self, animal, and object cleansing, along with some forms of house purifications. For yourself, combine daily showers with purifying visualizations and incantation. For pets, use an asperger (even a flower will work) to sprinkle them lightly with positively charged water. Similarly, there's nothing that says your wash water at home can't contain cleansing aromatics like lemon (which also neatly cuts dirt, both literal and figurative).

- *Smoke:* Typically from some type of incense, this process (called smudging) bears away any negative energy and disperses it to the winds. Smoke is a great alternative for items that are not waterproof. Just take care when using this in a group setting as, depending on the herbs chosen, it can cause allergic reactions. Common smudging herbs and resins include sage, cedar, lavender, sweetgrass, lemongrass, frankincense, and myrrh.

- *Fire:* A rather dramatic form of purification, ritually destroying something is one way to disperse the negativity therein. In some cases when an object has been seriously tainted using fire to purify it is a last resort. However, the smoke from a ritual fire can provide quality purification similar to that of smudging. We saw this second approach among the Celts, who used it to bless cattle.

- *Visualization:* A popular method because it's fairly simple and incredibly functional in nearly any setting. One approach is imagining any unwanted energy leaving a person, place, or thing in the form of dark goo that returns into the Earth's keeping.

- *Soil:* Sometimes objects are planted in rich soil to allow any unwanted energies to leach out, and the positive ones provided by a nurturing environment to enter. Obviously this method has limits (it's hard to plant a whole building, but you can landscape it!).

- *Salt:* A natural purifier and preservative, salt (or salt water) is another medium into which people have placed crystals and other objects. Soaking in a tub of salt water is a great way to cleanse your aura.

You'll likely come across other methods of cleansing and purifying in your travels. As with most magick, what makes one method "right" or "wrong" depends wholly on how meaningful they are to you. Choose what makes sense, what works, and stick with that approach unless circumstances do not allow it. Then go to your second favorite approach! For example, while it would be unwise to asperge my Book of Shadows with water, I can certainly smudge it with aromatic smoke. Better still, this second method lingers longer (the paper absorbs both the scent and energy pattern from the aromatic!).

Closure

Long is the road from conception to completion. —MOLIÈRE

Life is a circle. When one door closes another opens. That doesn't mean we forget about the door behind us, however. In fact, depending on exactly how that whole situation "went down" we may find ourselves feeling anything but settled in our new surroundings. Thus, a sense of closure is important to humans. Even the ever "go with the flow" neo-Pagan likes some form of definition! Granny GoodWitch likes it too. So how do you use magick·to help with closure-related matters?

I see it as having several potential applications. On a personal level, if there's a touchy situation involved, a last meeting in the constructs of sacred space is very beneficial to help healing along. While I realize there are times when it will be impossible to get everyone involved from a specific situation into a sacred setting (let alone wishing to partici-pate), there are ways around that issue. Namely, you can use symbolic items to pull things together.

Remote Closure Ritual

Let's put this into a specific scenario. Perhaps you've left a coven be-cause you and another person had a serious misunderstanding that led to overall group discord. You'd like to have some sense of closure be-tween you and him or her but cannot because communication has been cut off. In this case, you'd bring an image of that person into your space (or something to represent him or her) and a candle dedicated to him or her.

Place this candle near yours with another candle representing truth and Spirit between the two. Your personal candle and that of the other person's get lit from the flame of the Truth/Spirit candle. Then move to the East and begin an invocation like:

> *East:* Hail the rising sun. It is a new day. I welcome the winds of change into this sacred space. Bring with you the spirit of truth and understanding.
>
> *South:* Hail to the noon day sun that shines on the darkness. My path has changed. Bring with you the flames of illumina-tion to guide my soul.

West: Hail to the dusk, that represents endings and completion. Bring with you the healing waves of acceptance.

North: Hail to the night, which I reclaim. Bring with you rich
soils in which I will be nurtured and renewed.

Next, walk up to the candle representing that other person. Speak
whatever is in your heart but make it *constructive.* This is a healing process. Direct forgiveness, understanding, and your sincere desire for closure into that flame. When you feel spent, blow out the candle, take
yours in hand, and walk away until you're outside the circle. At that
point dismiss the guardians without looking back and blow out your
candle. The work is done.

I realize this example will not work for every situation, but it gives you a
good construct on which to build. Change your invocations, candles, and
other symbolic items according to your situation, but give yourself this
very important chance to at least create closure for yourself. If others accept the energy you send out, terrific. If not, it's not your karma anymore.

Color

*Often while reading a book one feels that the author would have preferred
to paint rather than write; one can sense the pleasure he derives from describing a landscape or a person, as if he were painting what he is saying,
because deep in his heart he would have preferred to use brushes and colors.*
—PABLO PICASSO

There are probably hundreds of books that provide you with color correspondences and tell you this symbolism is helpful in your magick. To

that foundation Granny would like to say, Don't forget about the psychology of color in your daily life! While you may not consider psychology and spirituality related, they are intimately connected. The power to make and change reality begins with thought, will, and focus (all conscious mental activity). Thus, utilizing the psychology of color in daily life will naturally improve the effects it has in your spiritual life.

Now, it's important to realize that since you're a unique individual you may find your psychological reaction to any particular color different from that of other people. To illustrate: Blue is considered a happy, peaceful color, and I find myself highly energized by it. Yes, it seems to improve my mood, but my energy levels also increase. This type of personal reaction should be carefully considered in how you apply color to any situation. To help yourself, keep a color chart where you make note of how various hues seem to affect you each day. For example, say you have to spend an hour or so in a predominantly green room—are you comfortable? Energized? Sleepy? Sad? Those are the kinds of reactions to pay attention to and make note of. Within a few weeks, you'll see trends appearing in your color chart that you can then mindfully utilize!

There are many easy ways to begin coloring your life in a manner that emphasizes your goals. The idea of "power ties or shirts" is one example that we already see. By extension, when you're feeling under the weather, bring pink highlights into your clothing and living space (i.e., being in the pink). Make sure that the item(s) you use here are seen regularly to stress the desired effect to your subconsious mind, and by extension your higher self.

Communication

There is more than a verbal tie between the words common, community, *and* communication . . . *Try the experiment of communicating,
with fullness and accuracy, some experience to another, especially if it be
somewhat complicated, and you will find your own attitude toward your
experience changing.* —JOHN DEWEY

If I had a dollar for every time what I said and what someone else *heard*
seemed like two completely different things I would be a very wealthy
woman. I see this particularly when two or more individuals are speaking from vastly different life experiences and constructs. To say the con-
fusion that results is frustrating is probably an understatement. The
inability to communicate ruins everything from relationships to global
peace treaties, because we keep trying to judge people from *our* vantage
point. How does one grasp the greater picture?

We can look to the ancients for a little advice here. Communication
is part listening, part using terms our companion(s) can understand, and
part a willingness to set aside our perceptions to see where the other
person is coming from. This is a very real trinity and a very tricky balancing act because (a) most people want to be right, (b) we all have
egos that fill in the blanks for us even when none exist, and (c) because
we are prone to human failing. The ancients knew this and turned to
various charms and talismans to help them fill in the communication
barrier with positive energy.

At the head of the list of components for achieving this goal we find
carnelian. Egyptians felt this stone cooled anger and encouraged peace
(it's pretty hard to communicate when everyone is shouting). More interesting still is the custom of kissing a ring of carnelian before a conversation, which seems to have arisen in Rome. Add to that the fact that
Mohammad himself wore an engraved stone, believing it to have great
virtue. I'd say that makes a very sound foundation for using carnelian in

modern communication spells, too, especially since it's relatively available and inexpensive.

Carnelian Communication Charm

As I mentioned earlier in this book, a charm needn't be anything more than a verbal empowering. However, in this case we're going to use words to "charge" a carnelian that we can then carry as a literal touchstone for speaking, listening, and understanding. You'll also need a piece of yellow cloth or a small yellow pouch for this charm (yellow is the color associated with communication).

To begin, set the carnelian in sunlight for three hours (to energize it with rational energies extending to body, mind, and spirit). Do likewise by the light of a full moon for three hours (to empower it with intuitive energy for body, mind, and spirit). Then, at midnight or noon on the following day, complete the charm by holding the carnelian in the palm of your hands and pouring your will into it, using an incantation like this one thrice:

> *Fill this stone within my hand*
> *With the power to understand*
> *When to my lips the stone is pressed*
> *All my words shall be blessed*
> *And when confusion is my fear*
> *Grant to me the power to hear!*
> *So be it.*

Slide the stone into the pouch and keep it in your purse or briefcase for ready access when you most need it. Touch the stone, mentally reciting the part of the incantation that applies, when you're in a situation requiring its energies.

Techno Communication Charm

For those of you who enjoy more modernized components and symbolism, go to a novelty store and look for a miniature telephone on a key ring (or a magnet or other small gift item). An alternative to the phone might be a computer. Both these symbols are strongly associated with today's intercommunications (and problems with them!). The key chain style is especially nice because it necessarily goes with you every time you leave the house.

You can use similar charging methods to those previously described for the carnelian. However, the incantation needs to change to reflect the item and its function. One example might be:

> *Little phone upon this ring*
> *Let my communications sing*
> *And like any tool for thoughts and words*
> *Let my meaning be clearly heard*

Now attach it to the rest of your keys, and you're set to go!

Courage

> *Courage is a special kind of knowledge: the knowledge of how to fear what ought to be feared and how not to fear what ought not to be feared.*
> —PLATO

Everyone has some level of fear, and in fact some fear is healthy. For example, being afraid of a hot stove keeps children from hurting themselves. But once we're past the learning process of what's good for us, and what is not, some fears remain. The fear of rejection, failure, disappointment, heights, dogs, confined spaces—and the list goes on!

Overcoming fear comes from honest confrontation of it. Is your fear realistic? If so, there's nothing to worry about other than finding a way to buttress yourself with courage, although that may not always be so easy. Here's one little spell that I've found helpful.

Bravery Buttress

For this spell you'll need a tea bag, preferably one whose flavor or aroma corresponds with the area in your life that requires more bravery. For example, if you need courage for your work, you might choose an orange tea (which stresses prosperity and diligence). Now, hold the tea bag in one hand and the tag at the end in the other. Slowly wind the string around the bag repeating this incantation three times:

> *In and around courage abounds*
> *When steeped in a cup—courage erupt!*
> *When taken within—the magick begins.*

Keep the tea bag somewhere safe until you need it, then just steep and enjoy to release the energy of the spell in your body, mind, and spirit.

If you examine your fears and find them unfounded, then you need to find ways of weeding them out of your mind and spirit. Part of the solution to this may be very mundane. The person who is afraid of heights, for example, takes lessons in rock climbing to work on the fear. Other people try hypnotism as a coping solution. When neither of these approaches work for you, or you'd like to try a spell to help, here's one with which to tinker:

Weeding Out Fear

For this activity all you need is a patch of weeds (if you don't have a yard, go to a nearby park where you can sit down on the ground among them). As you sit, imagine your fear like a black shadow that seeps out of your pores into the weeds. Name that fear specifically and mentally reflect on all the situations that bring your fear to the surface. When you feel like you're completely empty, reach down with a determined hand and pull the fear completely out. Hold that fear in your hands and tear it up completely, then stand up and release it to the winds. Walk away from that spot and don't look back (to do so subconsciously accepts the fear back).

Note that lifelong fears may require repeating this process numerous times to slowly drain them away, so be patient with yourself. There is nothing wrong with doing the activity once a month (working on the fear in mundane ways in between) until you're successful.

Coven or Solitary Practice

If one is lucky, a solitary fantasy can totally transform one million realities. —Maya Angelou

I vividly remember attending my first open circle. Watching was simply amazing. I hardly knew such as thing as Wicca existed and here I was observing dozens of witches all gathered together to celebrate. There was a comfort in seeing that group and knowing their ideas were very similar to my own. Being a social person, I hoped to become further involved in a group just like that one.

Life has its odd twists and turns, and that never happened. I ended up being a solitary practitioner. While there are times I bemoan that choice, in retrospect I know it's allowed me to stay outside of politics and group dynamics, and therefore to be more helpful to the community at large. Nonetheless, my Path is not yours. Making the choice between group or private practice is something that should be well considered.

Let's look to group practice first. In a group, you'll want people who share your vision of the Divine and magick, and with whom you're comfortable with their approaches to various workings. Any group that says you *must* do something that goes against your personal taboos or other strictures is one to avoid at all costs.

In exploring various groups, find out about the leadership and structure—is it consistent? Do people take turns preparing ritual? Do they have study groups on various topics so you can learn more? Do they follow a specific path or blend paths? While you're very unlikely to find any group that's perfect in every way, finding out as much as you can about it will provide a more complete picture of whether or not a group is right for you.

Joining a coven represents a commitment to each person in that group. You are a magickal cooperative, even when you're not getting along very well. You share energy and space with each other regularly, and when one person out of the whole is regularly absent, it leaves a "hole" in the energy pattern created. Therefore, be aware that there is a time investment involved with groups (and sometimes financial investments, too, if the group runs gatherings or hosts other events). Neither of these is a negative unless you're already time-challenged and over budget!

Meanwhile, solitary work stays wholly on your budget and time schedule. It does not, however, provide you with fellowship or mental and spiritual feedback from others. Also, a group can generally raise a lot more energy than can just one person working alone. On the other hand, there are no personality clashes and no need to adjust the way you work to compromise with others. The beauty of the solitary path is that it truly reflects your vision, but it does not give you structure or real discipline unless those are attributes you already possess.

The solitary life is more "fly by the seat of your broom" in that but for the Internet and friends who might be on a magickal Path, you really have to eke out the information you need for spells, rituals, meditations, or charms alone. The responsibility for any results from your efforts (for boon or bane) also lies totally with you. Balancing this against a group environment, you will always know if you're in the right physical, mental, and spiritual space for magick, while you can't always ensure that same preparedness in others.

As you can see from just this brief review, it may take you a while to make a choice. During that time, don't stop studying or working magick alone. Our lifestyle is such that it always offers flexibility. If you don't find you like working alone—find a group. If you don't like working with a group, find another one that appeals to your higher senses, or work alone. No matter what your decision, give a situation a fair chance. I suggest sticking with it for at least several months so that you know for certain (one way or the other) if you're in the right place, with the right people (even if the only person is you!).

Creativity

Creativity is piercing the mundane to find the marvelous.
—BILL MOYERS

A little ingenuity goes a long way in any witch's kit. If you could develop just one personal attribute that would improve all your magick, creativity ranks high on the list. It takes creativity to apply or adapt ancient symbols. It takes inventiveness to rework a ritual, and it certainly takes a bit of the muse to design visualizations and meditations! Be that as it may, there are many days when Granny GoodWitch finds that well of inspiration running pretty low if not totally dry. How do we refill and get things flowing again?

Well, we can look to the metaphors in our language as step one. How often have we heard of "artist's block," the need to "go with the flow," or about the "well being stopped up" when talking about our inventive self. Even in the aforementioned paragraph I spoke of creativity in liquid terms. So for my creativity magick I like to use water, juice, wine, or other liquids as a key component to the spell or ritual I'm using to get those juices running.

Berry Berry Creative

This potion begins with one large cup of orange juice (which inspires a little luck). To this add 3 strawberries, about 6 raspberries, and 6 blackberries. Whip it up in your blender (increases energy) while chanting:

> Fruit of the earth, bear fruit in me
> Bring to me creativity!

Drink with anticipation!

How do I go about choosing those liquids—again by the theme of the magick. For example, if I need more creativity in my relationship, mead is a good medium because it's been associated with love, inventiveness, and relationships for thousands of years. On the other hand, if I'm working on personalizing my divination system I might turn to beer or wine, which was sometimes used in fortunetelling efforts (in the belief that the spirits of the plants helped the task along). If the potion notion isn't pleasing, another alternative is making yourself a creativity charm.

Allspice Contrivance

Take a 3- by 3-inch square of yellow fabric, a yellow piece of yarn, and as many allspice berries as will fit inside (sachet style). Charge the berries by the light of a full moon for inventiveness, and place them inside, three at a time, adding an incantation like:

> *Inspiration come to me*
> *Berries gathered three by three*
> *By my will so mote it be!*

Carry this with you, but if you need inspiration to come quickly remove three of the berries and give them to the earth saying:

> *Inventiveness come now to me*
> *Release the magick three by three*
> *By my will so mote it be.*

Crystals

> *Crystals grew inside rock like arithmetic flowers. They lengthened and spread, added plane to plane in an awed and perfect obedience to an absolute geometry that even stones—maybe only the stones—understood.*
> —ANNIE DILLARD

There is no doubt in looking at modern marketing that crystals are "big business"—everything from tumbled stones for children to huge chunks of rock for interior design are available to please and delight us.

New Age fervor for them has given new energy to these wonders that humankind has loved for eons. Crystals entrance, fascinate, and endear themselves to us. All manner of glittery stones have been used since the dawn of time, for everything from trade goods to appeasing the gods! Magickally speaking, we find them used in talismans, charms, divinatory kits, and ritual clothing in places as far afield as Japan and the Native American frontier.

Since whole chapters in a variety of books have been dedicated to what crystals symbolize, I would rather stop to ponder how we are using them today while still being considerate of the Earth. Since uncovering stone is a natural byproduct of many other human activities, I don't really have strong ethical objections to buying crystals (except for those that are taken from nature preserves, rain forests, and other important resource areas). However, I might recommend trying to return something to nature for her gifts—a smattering of seeds, some other stones you no longer wish to use, an offering of water—just something that says "thank you." This keeps us mindful of our relationship with and responsibility toward nature. After all, stones are only tools—we are the enablers of the magick (and eventually one would hope we get past the need for such tools altogether).

That caveat aside, how many ways can you think of off the top of your head to apply crystals in your magick? Here's the list I came up with:

Crystal Clear Applications

- Placing elementally aligned stones around a room or sacred space to act as permanent protectors and guardians (and also to support the energy of the Guardians when called).

- Blessing and carrying various stones as charms, amulets, talismans, and fetishes.

- Tossing crystals into a well or moving water source with our wishes.

- Crushing stones and adding them to melted wax for candles (alternatively placing a small crystal in the base of a candle to improve the overall focus).

- Hanging crystals over windowsill gardens so the plants become further saturated by the stone's energies. (Note: This allows you to mix and mingle various vibrations for more refined result.)

- Planting crystals around your outdoor garden to protect the plants from animals or insects, and to support the energy within.

- Keeping a well-worn, flat stone in your shoe so that its energy "walks with you."

- Adding well-washed crystals to the bottom of bottles housing magickal potions (if the bottle is decorative the visual effect is quite lovely).

- Hanging crystals in windows so that as the sun shines through them, their energy disperses through the house.

- Leaving crystals on top of important papers or personal items, thereby allowing those things to absorb the energy.

- Putting crystals washed in very hot water into fish or lizard tanks to keep your pets healthier (no soap!).

And I'm sure I'm overlooking quite a few!

For the ardent reader and researcher, I highly suggest the book *Curious Lore of Precious Stones* by G. F. Kunz (Dover Publications) if you can find it. The information in this tome is invaluable in terms of getting close to first-source references. Scott Cunningham's *Crystal, Gem & Mineral Magic* is another option with less precise material, but it's well geared toward witches and neo-Pagans.

Curses

Curses are like young chickens, they come home to roost

—Arab proverb

A curse is a type of spell aimed at a specific person, group, or situation, typically to harm, vex, or balance the scales. As you might suspect, Granny has been asked many times about this ancient art and its ethics, especially when the proverbial shit has hit the fan in someone's life. And I'm going to tell you what I tell my students.

First, to understand curses, we must back up for one moment to reflect on the two-edged nature of magick. It certainly can be applied for good or ill, depending on the practitioner. However, when we combine this potential with the idea that whatever we send out comes back to us, curses seem to be rather unproductive for us in the long haul. The problem is that despite the apparent negatives, old spell books are filled to overflowing with curses that give us pause to consider them as a historically accurate methodology. Additionally, how can one know how to undo a curse if you have no clue as to how they're devised?

Perhaps our ancestors turned to curses because life was harsher then, and humankind's understanding of cause and effect was far less thorough than it is today. Perhaps it was also because people were far more superstitious. But at least in part curses were used because they were taught! Additionally, some of the curses come under a very "grayish" zone that could be considered karmic balancing, but I'm not wholly certain we have the wisdom to try to enact such things on the Universe's behalf!

So, my basic advice for those considering cursing is to think long and hard about it. In many ways cursing is like stooping to the level of someone else's negativity. Do you really want or need that? If you absolutely feel you must go to this extreme (and there are circumstances that press even the most well-meaning Pagans to the wall), there are a few precautions you can take.

1. Devise your curse in such a way that you *only* visit like for like (no embellishment allowed).

2. Be certain of who or what you're fighting, so you don't accidentally harm an innocent.

3. Never work from a place of anger. Cool off first, then pattern your magickal response.

Finally, and perhaps most important, allow Spirit to step in just in case there are parts of the equation you cannot see. This can be easily accomplished by adding what I call the "universal clause" to your spells, prayers, or rituals—namely: *for the greatest good* (or *the good of all*). Let's face it, what we think is right just simply isn't many times. Adding this phrase gives the Universe a chance to step in and direct the energy toward the best possible outcome.

Dating

What's nice about my dating life is that I don't have to leave my house. All I have to do is read the paper: I'm marrying Richard Gere, dating Daniel Day-Lewis, parading around with John F. Kennedy, Jr., and even Robert De Niro was in there for a day. —Julia Roberts

The dating game has changed a lot since I was young, and I really don't envy people in the singles scene. Spiritually-minded folk will probably want to meet those of a like mind to consider as potential dating partners. To that end, I suggest hanging out at New Age stores, magickal shops, natural cooperatives, and in the New Age section of a local bookstore. Typically these are some of the safest places to look and offer neutral territory on which to begin a conversation.

Overall, Granny Goodwitch's advice for dating is "Be careful, take it slow, and pack a double dose of magick in your pocket!" Here are three examples of the kind of spellcraft of which I speak.

Kiss Me Quick

Okay, you know you're going to meet someone toward whom you're highly attracted. Up till now that elusive first kiss hasn't come and you'd like to encourage it a bit. Magick can help! Your base component for this spell will be some lip balm. If you can get a flavor that you know your companion likes, or one that represents romance to you, all the better.

Charge the lip balm by the light of a full moon (which is much more romantic than daylight) saying:

> *When 'pon my lips my tongue does lick*
> *This balm sparks magick—so kiss me quick!*

Put this in a pocket or purse and apply it just before you meet your date.

Glamourous Glamoury

There are times when we all want to look and feel our best for a date. This glamoury pours positive energy into your aura that sizzles with appeal. I suggest standing while you enact this visualization. Begin by seeing yourself as you are right now, but there is a warm, sparkling white light overhead. Within that light are little sparks of color—all the hues of the rainbow. The colors you most need for confidence, comeliness, and creative communications spiral out from that light and begin to dance in your aura. Slowly they merge into your energy pattern until the image is that of a light shell of vibrant color all around you. You'll probably feel tingly or warm at this point, which tells you you're doing it right. This is the point at which you can leave for your date. When you feel yourself starting to wane a bit in terms of vibrancy, bring that image back to your mind to release more of the light-energy back into your body.

Meet 'n' Greet Amulets

These little amulets are perfect for social interactions, especially when meeting a lot of new people. You begin with a little container of breath mints (perfectly portable and mint improves communication!).

Since getting to know people touches on the conscious mind, I suggest charging these by sunlight. To this process you can add an incantation like:

> *Mint to make my words sweet*
> *With each new person I happen to meet*
> *When upon my tongue this candy tarries*
> *All conversations will be pleasant and merry!*

Slip the mints into your pocket and enjoy one before starting a new conversation.

As you can see there's a playfulness in dating spells that reflects the adventure at hand. You might also want to charge any protective items you carry for these encounters, too, for obvious reasons. While I would wish that there were no such thing as date rape and other abuses of human sexuality, these are a part of the reality of the world in which we live. Be wise; be prepared.

Dedication/Initiation

Most of us serve our ideals by fits and starts. The person who makes a success of living is one who sees his goal steadily and aims for it unswervingly. That's dedication.
                                                                    —CECIL B. DE MILLE

People frequently ask Granny if it's "necessary" to undergo some type of formal dedication or initiation into the Craft to be a "real" witch. My answer is that while it doesn't hurt, it's not a necessity. Being a witch is something that comes from within. The dedication or initiation is something external that illustrates the internal reality.

Let me back up for a minute. Dedication is a little different from initiation, and it's good to understand the two in context. A dedication is something that can be done alone. It's simply a moment in which a person goes before the Powers and expresses a heartfelt intention to study a specific path. It may include a personal oath (a level of commitment in time and energy), and it may also include the declaration of a chosen magickal name, and acknowledgment of a Patron or Patroness deity.

By comparison, an initiation is group oriented. It often follows a period of study with that specific group (a year and a day is one time frame that's customary). In this manner, the group gathers together to welcome a coven member and also acknowledge his or her spiritual progress communally. In some instances an initiation may be offered to someone at an open circle setting if that person chooses to be a solitary pratitioner but still wants a public acknowledgment of his or her Path. As with the dedication, this may be a time when a person declares a magickal name or God/dess that he or she intends to follow.

Now, having said all that, I do feel there is real value in either process. Humans are creatures of ritual. We use ritual as a way of consummating something—of making it real and more fulfilled in our mind and heart. In this case, you're making a promise to yourself and Spirit here, and accepting all your potential as a spiritual and magickal being. That's a lot to internalize, and it's one of the key moments in your personal progression.

Taking the step toward dedication or initiation should, therefore, be carefully considered. Don't let anyone rush you into it. In the meanwhile just keep your heart and soul open. Feed them both with your ongoing studies and practices. You'll know when the time is right.

Diplomacy

Diplomacy is a game of chess in which the nations are checkmated.
—KARL KRAUS

No, you cannot turn Johnnie into a toad just because he pissed you off. No, no...not a newt either! For one, such practices are very passé (come on, get creative), and for another, a healthy dose of diplomacy is far less stressful on your karmic bank account! Those of you who have chosen coven life will find the art of diplomacy doubly useful. There's nothing better for successful group dynamics than someone who can keep a level head and act as a mediator.

Bear in mind that diplomacy encompasses the skills of communication, awareness, adaptation, and temper control (anger management). You need sound communication skills to be able to talk to everyone involved using terms they all understand equally. You need awareness to realize when one party or the other is getting too riled up for effective communication. Adaptation lets you react quickly to the changing tides, and keeping your own temper in check helps you maintain overall control. Definitely consult those headings in this book for ideas to get you started.

Before you go into the proverbial lion's den, however, it doesn't hurt to enact a little magick (if nothing else, it provides moral support).

Diplomacy Divination

This divination helps you predetermine where the major problems lie in negotiation. Begin by lighting a yellow candle. Have a paper and pen handy along with a coin, and any objects that can represent the individuals or situation at hand. I've chosen a simple binary divination system as it provides important yes and no answers. For example, focus your mind on Person A. Ask if Person A was the main individual holding up a resolution. Toss the coin. Heads is yes and tails is no. Next you can ask a series of other questions to clarify the situation, based on what you already know. Use the information you gather as a starting point in the negotiations. Using our previous illustration, if the results indicate Person A is a key player, you might want to consult that individual privately before going into a tense group meeting to see what can be worked out.

Ambassadorial Amulet

The saying "Don't shoot the messenger" didn't come into modern usage by happenstance. Very often it's the guy or gal waving the white flag that gets shot at (figuratively or literally). So if you'd like a portable token to take with you, this one might prove ideal.

I've chosen the eye agate as the medium for this amulet for several reasons. The eye patterning implies intuitiveness and vision. Additionally, these stones were commonly used as protective devices (to turn away the "evil eye"). This combination is very well suited symbolically and historically to the focus here. I don't even think you really need an incantation unless you'd like to give the amulet activating words to turn it on just before negotiations begin (thereby preserving energy until it's most needed).

If you choose an activating phrase, try good affirmations like *success, peace, prevail,* or something else that relates directly to the situation. Speak that word into the stone three times (the fourth time turns it "off").

By the way, if the people involved are of a magickal ilk, perhaps you can talk them into holding these talks in sacred space to encourage pure motivations.

Doubt

The only limit to our realization of tomorrow will be our doubts of today.   —FRANKLIN D. ROOSEVELT

Doubt is nearly as destructive as fear in every corner of life. When we find our faith failing, our magick will also fail. We must trust in it because trust ties into will, and will resides at the helm of our Craft (thus the phrase "by my will" comes up so readily in spellcraft).

Now, being that none of us is enlightened yet, we still have burrs that make sitting in our skin uncomfortable. Self-doubt, doubt of others, or doubts about a situation are among them. Some of these doubts (as some fears) are a very *good* thing. They keep us from blindly rushing in where angels fear to tread. But when unfounded doubts, or those stemming from insecurities, hold you back, try a little magick to bolster yourself.

Certainty Cooler

This potion is designed not only to improve your sense of certainty but also to keep your head cool and clear until the situation resolves itself. The components you need to gather:

> 1 quart water
> 6 tea bags
> ¼ lemon (sliced)
> ½ orange (sliced)

Place these in a plastic or glass container in the sunlight just as you would to make sun tea. The tea here provides the foundation of assurance, while the lemon adds clarity and the orange determination. Let the ingredients steep in sunlight (to charge with conscious, logical energies) until it's heady and as potent as you personally like.

Next, take out the fruit and tea bags and let the tea chill in the refrigerator. This provides you with the ability to stay calm, cool, and collected. Each morning (or several times a day, if you can take it with you) enjoy a cup that you bless by saying:

> *Tea for assurance, in my mind and my heart*
> *Lemon for clarity—all confusion depart!*
> *Orange for fortitude, strength and peace*
> *By my will—the magick release!*

Sip slowly and let the energy fill you from toe to head.

Confidence Charm

I like to use dry spinach as the key component in this charm (you can get it in freeze-dried form or dry it yourself) because of the Popeye cartoons. Not only did spinach give Popeye strength, but that strength in turn no doubt provided him with greater confidence to tackle things he previously thought impossible. Now, while this symbolic value for spinach is rather modern, it's one to which most people can immediately relate, which therefore empowers the magick.

To create the charm you need about ¼ cup of the dried spinach and a red pouch or swatch of cloth into which you can bundle the spinach. Energize the pouch/sachet saying:

> *The strength of many bundled within*
> *When released to the winds, the spell begins*
> *To my heart, to my mind—confidence direct*
> *Away from me—doubt reflect*

Carry the pouch with you, sprinkling out just a little bit of the spinach to the winds when you most need it. Do not let the pouch get completely empty. Refill and recharge it when it gets down to about ½ full.

Dreams

Your vision will become clear only when you look into your heart. Who looks outside, dreams. Who looks inside awakens. —CARL JUNG

Dreams can be interpreted many ways. Some are simply replays of a day—little bits of information that your mind tucked away and is only now getting to internalize. Other dreams stem from worries, fears, wonders, and fantasies. Others still might contain tidbits of foreknowledge, or perhaps even a message from Spirit. The big questions for most people are—how does a person determine what dreams are important, and how exactly does one go about encouraging "spiritually" oriented dreams?

Let's consider the first question. For one thing, *all* dreams are important psychologically. Dreaming is a natural process for our mind, and something that's required—even if you don't happen to remember what you dream. There are some telltale signs that will help you identify dreams to which you should be paying specific attention. They include:

- A recurring dream (typically one that you've had more than three times).

- A dream that evokes a strong, involuntary physical or emotional reaction.

- A dream whose memory stays with you throughout the remainder of the day, or continues to come to mind days or weeks afterward.

- A dream that seems incredibly real, to the point that upon waking you still felt like you were dreaming (or could still see images from the dream in the periphery).

- A dream that connects to or explains something important that's happening in present reality.

If you experience one or more of those indicators it's time to get out your dream diary and make notes. Compare your insights to those of two or three of your favorite dream interpretation books. See what baseline symbolism begins to emerge.

But what about those of us who have trouble dreaming or who would like to manifest specifically spiritual dreams? Well, Granny GoodWitch has some good tidbits for both situations. First, I highly recommend bedtime affirmations (simply repeating something like "I will remember" as you fall asleep, which has the additional benefit of helping hone your conscious memory too!). Second, keep some type of notepad, pen, or tape recorder readily available. The details of our dreams tend to slowly disappear from our memory the longer we're awake. So, if you have even a small glimmer of a dream and write it down right away, it will help you in the interpretive process. Third, look to components that witches and Cunning Folk have used for eons. Herbs to encourage spiritual or prophetic dreams include:

- Roses
- Jasmine
- Bay
- Lemongrass
- Marigold
- Mistletoe
- Cinnamon
- Thyme

Crystals and minerals associated with dreaming include:

- Azurite
- Moonstone
- Silver
- Amethyst

To this foundational component list you can also add various edibles that encourage spirituality and psychism like:

- Corn
- Coconut
- Wine
- Olives
- Honey
- Fish

Mix and match as you see fit into spells, charms, potions and notions. For example, you could make a small sachet filled with rose petals, cinnamon, and some tiny moonstones to put under your pillow. Or, perhaps make a dream catcher with amethyst beads and a bundle of bay leaves for over your bed.

What's most important here is that you take time to pay attention to your dreams and give the Spirit within and without a chance to speak to you through them. See, we have a larger faith factor in our dreamtime that allows us to accept what we see there as truly possible. This faith factor, when it flows over into your magick, is a powerful tool. The more you work and interact with your dreamscapes, the more I believe you'll find the positive energy from that experience empowering your soul. Or at least that's been my experience.

Dare to dream... then take those dreams into reality and make them come true!

Drums

Natives who beat drums to drive off evil spirits are objects of scorn to smart Americans who blow horns to break up traffic jams.

—MARY ELLEN KELLY

In the broad-based neo-Pagan community, drummers are the fastest growing subsection. Why is that? I think perhaps we can find our answers by looking at the ways drums were used historically. In a tribal setting, drums became the heartbeat of the community. They called people together around the sacred fire, they rang out with messages, and they provided music by which one could dance, listen to, and reconnect with both the Divine and the rest of the village.

Then and now, the sound of the drum becomes a focal point. If our attention is all in one place, it becomes easier to bridge the gaps between people and even dimensions. The sound becomes our walkway and guide. Nonetheless, it is not everyone's path to be a drummer anymore so that it's everyone's path to be a Druid or a Witch. While I feel this is a very valuable tool to include in the witch's kit, there's a difference between using the drum personally, and it becoming a way of magick unto itself.

The drum has a very distinctive spirit—it's one focused on community, on the good of All. The drummer's Path, therefore, is one where his or her circle (community, tribe, etc.) becomes a focus for servicing the All. Additionally, the person walking this path utilizes the drum as the main tool/component in all his or her magick (much as a folk witch uses folklore).

Outside this construct, those wishing to use the drum as an additional item for various types of magick, the first necessity will be finding the right drum for you. They come in all sizes, numerous shapes, and a wide variety of tones. Some are much more difficult to learn than others, and *all* require that you try them out (hands on) to determine if you've discovered a good spiritual partner. How? By listening to your heartbeat with your hands on its surface. Tap the top of the drum lightly once, then again more loudly. How does that feel measured against the sound and pace of your heart? If it's right you'll know it without a doubt.

As for utilizing this implement once you've found one? Here are a few ideas:

- Drum quietly during meditation, using your breath to help you pace the beat.

- Drum the quarters, adjusting the sound and rhythm to honor the elements as you reach each region.

- Drum as an offering to Spirit.

- Drum to greet the dawn or dusk.

- Drum to mark the opening or closing of a ritual or spell.

If you decide to take your drum to a gathering, take care to remember that you've moved into a communal space. Here your task is a little different. Rather than play at a personal pace or volume, now you need to mingle with the energies around you. Honor that sacred space and every person there by stopping to listen before ever putting a hand on your drum. Attune yourself to the energy around you, then join gently.

Earth Magick

Treat the Earth well: it was not given to you by your parents, it was loaned to you by your children. We do not inherit the Earth from our Ancestors, we borrow it from our Children. We are more than the sum of our knowledge, we are the products of our imagination.

—Ancient proverb

There are two ways of thinking about Earth Magick. First is the magick that we enact specifically for the planet to facilitate its ongoing well-being. The second is magick that's centered around natural objects. Since we'll look at the second category under the topic of "Green Magick," Granny would like to address those spells, rituals, and other spiritual methods we devise specifically for Gaia.

While most people would never think of just randomly tossing their trash on a friend's lawn, for hundreds of years that's pretty much what humankind has been doing to the earth. At some point we stopped thinking of the Earth as sacred and began treating it as our dominion, not seeing the long-term effects of such neglect until recently. Nonetheless it seems that some of our wise ancestors left us clues as to how we should think about and treat the earth both substantively and spiritually.

As early as the third century, the Greek philosopher Porphyry spoke

about the trees having souls. Saint Anthony told us that nature was
God's "open book" and Saint Francis basically became the patron of
ecologists through his ardent love and care for wildlife. It was he who
spoke of Mother Earth as nourishing humans (and I suspect he meant
more than our bodies!). And these people are not alone. Numerous
well-respected figures, from Jesuit priests and European alchemists to
nineteenth-century writers and artists like Henry David Thoreau, were
trying to define this great gift. It just took us a while to really see and
hear their message.

Finally, in 1982 the United Nations created a special charter that lays
out ways of safeguarding the environment. In 1983 and 1987, the religious sector followed suit when the World Council of Churches focused
on creation's integrity, and Pope John Paul told Catholics everywhere
that human "dominion" over the Earth was not absolute and that we
must use this treasure wisely. Sadly, at the turn of the millennium we
find some of that focus blurred behind other social issues and in some
cases even a slacking on environmental laws. Granny feels (quite
bluntly) that this is a travesty against which any person of sound ethical standards should fight with any means possible. Our children deserve a whole Earth, not whatever remnants we choose to leave behind.

While not everyone is a political activist, there are many small ways
you can fight for our planet. Watch for companies who abuse her resources and boycott their products (hitting the pocketbook is often
very successful). Also watch for those political figures who support
ecological necessities like finding alternative, clean fuel sources and *vote*
for them. Beyond these kinds of things, don't forget about the power in
a witch's kit! Create spells, rituals, charms, and meditations that direct
their energy back to she who sustains us all: the Earth.

For example, a simple visualization that I add to many pre-bed rites is
that of the Earth being bathed in a sphere of white-blue light. The little specks of light reach beyond the atmosphere, collect negativity and
toxins, and then remove both, leaving behind only natural beauty. This
visualization does two things—it provides me with the image of a
whole world (the power to make and change reality really does begin in

our thoughts). It also extends healing, helpful energy to the Spirit of Gaia who needs our service just as surely as her body does. This is the kind of activity that I encourage all practitioners to take part in at least once a month, if not once a week. Earth certainly deserves that much of our time and energy.

Before closing this section, Granny would like you to ponder these things:

- You cannot touch a blade of grass without affecting a star.

- The same water that fell on Moses is still part of our water system today.

- As you breathe right now, the molecules of air that everyone in the world has also taken into their vital systems within the last two weeks is part of that breath.

- You must love something to make it whole. How much do we each love our world?

Perhaps a Native American writer said it best (and I apologize that I do not recall the person's name) when he said: Let us all come to know the Earth by one name—home!

Elders, Teachers, Priest/esses

Teachers open the door, but you must enter by yourself.
—CHINESE PROVERB

True to most Cunning Folk, not everything I share with people is necessarily "spiritual"—it comes under the heading of food for thought.

This is one of those subjects, and one about which I don't pad the corners. In my years in the magickal community I've watched a lot of our elders, teachers, and leaders get completely burned out. This happens in part because these people care so much that they put personal needs on the back burner. And while we can't necessarily help that drive to serve, there is one problem that we can help with—namely giving back equally to their energies.

Those that serve need service. Most people who have heard me speak publicly are probably tired of that last sentence, but it remains my mantra until I see substantive changes in our community. There are a lot of needy people in the world, and when we're in need we often overlook the very person assisting us. That's normal—but later, when that need has passed how do *you* say thank you? What do *you* give back to that person, and to the All? How do you complete the circle? These are very important questions and ones that I pose to myself too.

If we don't take care of the people who have earned our respect and gratitude through honorable actions and ongoing dedication, it reflects negatively on our ethics, especially to those looking from the outside in. While the "world" may still be in a disposable mindset (when something is worn out—just replace it), we are a community focused on nurturing, sustenance, and recycling. In terms of people this means using our human resources wisely—sustaining them, nurturing them, and sharing what we learn from them with others (thereby recycling the material). How exactly? In any way you can! Give them a hug; offer a backrub, make them a meal; clean their house or do yard work—free up their hands and time so they can continue their efforts for the good of All.

But don't stop there. We need to keep the wheel of giving and receiving rolling or it will inevitably become flat (and likely run over a few good people in the process). If you remember to keep the words *balance* and *reciprocity* in your thoughts, words, and actions, you'll be doing very well indeed.

Along the same lines, it's important that we take great care in how our respected titles get used. Reading one book, leading one ritual, or taking an online course in the Craft does *not* give anyone the right to call himself or herself a Priest or Priestess. While we each play that role on a personal level, that title has *group* implications and it's one that's earned. Likewise, adding shamanic practices to one's path does *not* make you a Shaman. Such a distinction takes years, if not a lifetime, of study and practice. When we misuse these titles (either out of ignorance or ego) we dishonor those who have, by rights, earned those designations.

Why get so uppity about a title? There are many good reasons. For one, it makes things very confusing for people outside our community, and our novices, to know who's who and if that person is trustworthy. For another, titles like teacher, elder, and Priest imply a well-deserved privilege and right—making any such claim solely to bolster a public image strikes me as deplorable, and something against which we should speak out. It robs our true leaders (many of whom you don't even see because they are working quietly behind the lines) of the honor they are due.

What do we do about those who set themselves up in ivory towers? My advice is to first confront the individual and ask how they came by their position. You have every right, especially if you are thinking of joining a group, to know your leader's training, get references, and follow up on those references. Research and networking are among the most powerful tools we have available to us.

Speaking of networking, if you find someone who is really "out there" you can share that information with other people in your area by networking. Now, by "out there" I don't mean you disagree with their magickal constructs or personal politics. I mean things like:

- Running a coven or study group under false pretenses (like claiming training or lineage they do not have).

- Claiming to have the most powerful (and 100 percent successful) form of magick.

- Calling themselves a witch (or Shaman, Druid, etc.) in an effort to manipulate people.

- Making promises of incredibly effective curses, potions, etc., for equally incredible service fees.

- Requiring a coven or study group member to do something that goes against personal ethics or they cannot be in the group and so forth.

All of these types of activities send up a *huge* warning flag in my mind if not a *stop* sign. Document everything you find out from that point forward and then share it with individuals and groups alike.

Please do so without becoming a gossip—bear in mind the goal is to help, not harm. You don't need to backbite—just present the documented facts and let individuals draw their own conclusions. I've seen this done on several Pagan websites very successfully. By so doing, you give people an opportunity to weed out the weekend warriors, Wiccan-wannabes, and ego ring-kissers in favor of those who are truly walking the walk.

Elements

> *Nature that fram'd us of four elements,*
> *Warring within our breasts for regiment,*
> *Doth teach us all to have aspiring minds.*
> —CHRISTOPHER MARLOWE

Shamanism, Witchcraft, Druidry, and many other metaphysical belief systems work with the powers of earth, air, fire, and water. The wise witch's school of magic is no different. These four elements (bound together by Spirit) constitute an amazing storehouse of symbolism and power that we can apply to any need or goal. So, if you'll forgive a momentary pun—"Let's get element-ary!"

Since dozens of books have already provided you with more crystal, animal, and plant correspondence lists and elemental associations than you'll need for ten incarnations, and others still have talked about the beings that abide within those elements, I thought Granny would give you a slightly different look at things. More specifically, let's go back to the basics and what we can do with just good old-fashioned Earth, air, fire, and water.

Water

Rain water, dew, spring water, sweet water, and water mixed with natural oils or juices has been used in blessings and spellcraft for thousands of years in numerous traditions. Pilgrims to Mecca dip prayer beads in water, while Germans sanctified their fields up until the twelfth-century by asperging them with water. Macedonians brought water to their courtyards for good fortune, Celts sprinkled water from a broom to invoke rain, and in both Assyria and Europe, water-washed stones were used as part of curatives.

As an aside, well water was sometimes used for all these purposes, but more often for wishing. By comparison salt water (ocean water) was used to banish sickness, probably because the salt itself is a preservative. But let's not stop there—what about water's alternative forms: tears, sweat, ice, fog, and steam?

Tears, to me, represent specific emotions. So if you gather a few, and place them into a beverage, you can internalize the positive emotions. Otherwise, give them to the earth to bury negative feelings. Sweat is closely related to tears in that it's physical and very personal. Use small amounts of this to mark personal space and items. And before you say *ewwwwwww*, remember it's a much nicer alternative than the substances called for in some of the old methods!

Ice is one of my favorite mediums, because the water molecules have slowed (thereby causing the solid state). Water in this form is excellent for protection, cooling anger, freezing bad luck, etc. Conversely, if you put something into ice and then melt it—you symbolically release it from "limbo." By the way, a bit of folklore says if you wish to remember something forever—write it with your finger on ice.

Foggy nights make for a marvelous time to work magick because they invoke a feeling of timelessness. Lastly, steam is akin to smoke in that it rises to the winds with our wishes and prayers. Potpourri water that's steaming might well be used to bless a sacred space or the fragrant steam can be fanned upon participants before a ritual begins.

Earth

The planet's soil has been used for eons in magick. It was quite common at one time to place a sick person into the Earth (head above ground) as a type of mock death. When they rose, their sickness stayed in the earth! Other similar methods included spitting into the earth and covering it (to bury the illness), or putting healing herbs into a person's footprint. Oddly enough, if you gather soil from that same footprint it's said to help with love spells!

As with water, there are several forms of Earth to consider for your magick including clay, dust, sand, and mud. Clay has two applications. The first comes in the form of image magick in that you can shape the clay however you wish, like a poppet. The second would be for beauty or image magick, since rich clays are often used to enrich the skin.

Sand has some properties similar to clay, in that it can be shaped when wet (and then can be taken out to sea with the next tide). When I'm stressed out, I like to hold warm sand in my hands and let it slowly trickle out (taking my tensions with it). And, of course, Native Americans and Tibetans both practice sand painting as a meditation and form of healing.

Dust when gathered from specific places is considered protective (especially graveyard dust—in practice symbolizing victory over the grave). In some areas of the world dust was used for divination, either by casting it and watching its movements, or by patterns on its surface.

Finally, mud is a blend of Earth and water, giving it a strong healing quality. Dab a bit of mud on a bug bite—it really helps. Beyond that, wash away some mud when you need to clear up a situation!

Air

The wind has long been connected with Spirit (or spirits) because it's so elusive. In the Far East it wasn't uncommon to listen to the winds for portents. In the West it was typically observed as a weather indicator, and sometimes used as part of healing spells.

Where the first water and Earth offered us various forms, the winds offer directions. Those moving from the East provide hopeful energies for new beginnings and improved communications. Those from the South are energetic and passionate. Those from the West touch on matters of the heart, and those from the North manifest improved finances and foundations.

In terms of applying the wind—you can hang your clothing in the winds from a specific direction to charge and refresh it. Or cast herbs, flower petals, or other natural, light items to the winds with your wishes. Stand in the wake of a wind and let the air's energy fill you!

Fire

Fire is considered the most difficult element to work with simply because you can get burned (literally). The historical applications for this element were numerous, including divination (pyromancy), encouraging love and luck, weather magick, and protection. It's interesting to note the last use in that tree limbs struck by lightning (a type of fire) were kept in homes to safeguard against lightning and fire (because "lightning never strikes twice").

Thanks to modern conveniences we have several forms of fire to consider: the stove, the hearth, candles, and lamps or flashlights. I realize these last two options are more metaphorical, but for those who live in small spaces using a flashlight can be a great alternative that's safe. I might also suggest ashes as a potential "fire" component, since they are formed as a result of fire, and house all that energy within.

The stovetop works fine as a source for cooking up magick, while the oven can bake energy to perfection. The hearth (fireplace) can be used for scrying and spellcraft (typically the latter includes burning something so the smoke carries your wishes upward). Candles create an ideal ambiance for meditation and other magickal workings, not to mention being a fantastic spell component (readily available and cheap). Lamps and flashlights "warm up" so you can dab them with aromatic oil to release energy into an area. And finally, ashes can be added to power pouches and herbal blends when you want to add fire's vibrations without actually adding fire.

Enlightenment *(Spiritual Progress)*

Do not think you will necessarily be aware of your own enlightenment.
—Dogen

Granny finds it very interesting that for all our talk about magickal practices and ideologies, we rarely talk about spirituality in the equation. I think this might be because we're using different words for that concept, or perhaps because we find it hard to verbalize the deeper internalizations and awarenesses that our spiritual path brings. While there are probably some people who have missed this element in their development altogether, I think most people walking a magickal Path are trying to move forward toward adepthood.

But then the question becomes, what exactly is an adept? I mean, every time we reach a new platform in our growth, there's always another ahead! In that realization alone is part of our answer. True spiritual adeptness comes from recognizing that life is a classroom filled with ongoing opportunities to learn and transform. It need not stop until we do!

Another clue on what it means to be an Adept comes from the term's roots—specifically *adeptus* means arrival. We are all arriving somewhere in our spiritual lives every day. Even small steps still mark forward movement—but all too often we don't see them because our attentions are elsewhere. It's time to pause for a moment and really begin to see those "arrivals" and honor them in our lives.

Since each person's path is unique, rather than give you specific advice on becoming adept, I'd like to provide you with some signs that you're heading in the right direction. Over the years, these are the earmarks I've seen in people who have become our honored elders, teachers, and leaders...those whose lives are a shining example to all:

Signs of Spiritual Progress

A person who is making positive spiritual progress and showing signs of adepthood typically exhibits the ability to:

- Balance the mundane and mystical, the temporal and eternal in both thought and action.

- Show honor, gratitude and respect to others, Spirit, and to self when it's well deserved.

- Be truthful even when it's a difficult truth.

- Show strength and weakness, aptitude and failure, and remain wholly peaceful within.

- Walk the walk, twenty-four hours a day, seven days a week.

- Give something substantial back to his or her art or community.

- Live life as an act of worship.

- Gauge spiritual progress by milestones in the heart (as opposed to measuring against others).

- Be thoughtful, improvisational, aware, alert, responsible, graceful, and prayerful not just as needs arise, but as a way of life.

- Go with the flow, accepting the wonder of new circumstances and challenges as they arise.

- Stand his or her ground when circumstances call for firmness.

- Work for wholeness in self, others, and the Earth.

- Simplify.

- Offer assistance and insights freely.

- Work for the All, without the need for title or recognition.

We spoke a little already about the respect due our leaders, and this last point is one of particular importance. Every "old soul" that I've ever met never felt the need for bravado or fanfare. He or she seemed wholly comfortable with anonymity, and when someone recognized a bit of wisdom—they just smile, nod knowingly, and rejoice in the awakening in you. While this trait and the others I've listed are certainly not the whole picture, it's a good place to begin. And remember—when you reach milestones and see that shift in yourself, by all means celebrate doing so. It is something in which to rejoice.

Ethics and Morals

All virtue is summed up in dealing justly. —ARISTOTLE

Whoa...trying to talk to neo-Pagans about ethics and morals is like herding cats. In a vision-based culture (which witches are part of) it's very hard to get anyone to agree on even minor points, let alone the biggies like what constitutes right, wrong, black, and white. The line in the sand shifts for each individual walking this Path. So how do we begin to gauge our own ethical standards, let alone those of others, without becoming judgmental?

This is a real worm can, but one that Granny will open anyway (we do, after all, tend to have our opinions on everything). First I'd like to state outright that I think we desperately need some type of black-and-white outlines, if for no other reason than so people trying to learn about neo-Paganism have some type of construct. Better still, those constructs help novices and teachers too! Before you object, remember that having outlines doesn't mean you can't have a lot of personalization and even color outside the lines from time to time. Constructs have some built-in flexibility to those who think out of the box!

So what do I consider the constructs of our ethics? Mostly things that come from common sense. For example, pain hurts. Some pain is avoidable (to self, to others, to the Earth), some is not. Avoid the pain that is avoidable! Perhaps that sounds overly simplistic, but if we're endeavoring to remain aware and thoughtful every moment of every day, then our spiritual instincts have a greater chance to interact with and affect reality.

Other ethical constructs? Be nice to each other, be good caregivers for our planet, and keep Spirit as a constant companion. Even when you have to take a stand or point out a wrong, it need not become a proverbial pissing match. I can't tell you how often a minor "he said–she said" in a coven ended up in an all-out brawl and damaged friendships for years to come. This isn't only silly—it's immature and unenlightened. If we are spiritual beings having a human experience, this is one of those times to let our spiritual nature guide the helm! Similarly, in our life on this Earth, if each of us strives to leave our spaces a little better than when we arrived, the results become geometric.

Finally, Spirit is a great ethical guide. That little voice within knows what's truly right or wrong in the greater scheme of things. Spirit encompasses the pattern of wholeness, which is exactly what we all seek. If we begin to recognize that pattern, and make it part of ourselves, we will naturally live accordingly. This is an example of "as within, so without" on an intimate level.

Listening to Spirit

When I find I have a difficult ethical choice to make, and when I don't know what is the best or right thing, I often take to prayer and meditation to sort it out. For whatever reason, Spirit seems to speak most clearly when we are still. So for this activity I strongly recommend finding a place where you won't be interrupted, and one that has as little manmade noise as possible. Such noises are not only nonproductive to the activity, but tend to disrupt the natural and magickal patterns in our auras.

Once you've secured a quiet place, sit in whatever position you normally adopt for meditation or prayer. Close your eyes and begin breathing deeply and evenly. Allow your breaths to become all-connected (the end of one breath smoothly becomes the beginning of another).

Next, slowly delete various sounds from your awareness. Begin with the wind, any birds, a barking dog. Focus inward. Listen only to your breath and your heartbeat. A little at a time, diminish your awareness of those sounds. Listen as if from a very long distance away until they are all but gone. This is the point at which to mentally or verbally pose your question to Spirit. Be clear and concise, then stop and just listen.

Be patient. Answers don't always come quickly. Also be aware that Spirit relays information to people in a form to which they're most likely to respond. For example, if you're a highly visual person an image might pop into your mind. It could be a literal one, or something symbolic. Pay attention to that, but don't try to hold on to it—there may be more yet to come. Those who have strong audio leanings might hear a whisper, or music, or another type of sound that provides guidance.

If you're outdoors you may discover movement among various creatures or the winds conveying a message. Don't automatically eliminate that possibility. Spirit's fingerprint resides in nature too! When you're done, make sure you take notes of your experiences and read them over in the days, months, and even years ahead. I have generally found that such messages are timeless, and hold much wisdom in many situations.

As one might expect, Spirit is pretty big—and very diverse. Thus our community is as well. Nonetheless, beneath it all there are underlying truths that await our discovery. As we find those threads of truth, we can begin to weave together a fabric of ethics, and slowly create a tapestry to which we can return again and again for more perspectives.

Etiquette

Good manners have much to do with emotions. To make them ring true,
one must feel them, not merely exhibit them. —AMY VANDERBILT

Throughout the neo-Pagan community there are some basic ethical guidelines that you can follow to make yourself and others feel more welcome and comfortable. While we are living in times when common courtesy seems to have gone by the wayside, these little things mean a lot, especially to responsible spiritual seekers. So, Granny would like to do something that all grannies do—give you some hints on maintaining good spiritual etiquette.

To begin, don't randomly tinker with other people's magickal tools. The rule of "ask first" is always best. Doing otherwise is kind of like randomly opening people's drawers on your first visit to their home. It's a breach of privacy and may inadvertently affect the energies associated with that item.

Second, in a festival setting, be very respectful of the community fire. Poking and prodding the wood often results in sparks that can set things on fire, or burn exposed skin. Likewise, don't toss garbage or even herbs into the fire without checking with a designated fire tender. The chemicals in some garbage can be volatile and the herbs can cause allergic reactions for some participants.

The community fire is one spot at festivals where people gather to dance, sing, and sometimes observe entertainers. Thus it's polite to take private conversations elsewhere. Also if you have restless children who are playing nearby and making noise, it's nice to move them too. Trust me—your fellow attendees will appreciate the consideration.

Speaking of children: Parents, please make sure your children have adequate coverage when you cannot be with them. While we are a tribe, your children are *your* responsibility. Especially in a large group or gathering, not everyone can be trusted to be wise or to know your child's habits and needs. As the future of our Craft, our children deserve more consideration than we give them sometimes because we want to have "fun." So my best advice is either take someone along with you for extra help, hire a sitter, or find a way for your children to participate fully in the events you attend so they're both involved and safely occupied (with proper supervision).

In our interactions with each other, another issue that comes up for me regularly is whether to hug or shake hands upon introduction. We often assume everyone hugs—and that's simply not the case. There are people who have suffered abuses in our community along with those who have taboos against touching anyone but family members. There are also those who simply aren't "touchy feely" people, who find hugging uncomfortable. Since not all of these folks have a "no hug" button, it's good to ask preferences.

Another good example along the same lines is the taking of photographs. There are a lot of people who, because of jobs or family, cannot have their pictures from festivals or circles just floating around in the public sphere. Then, too, some people just dislike having their pictures taken. So much is this the case that many festival coordinators have all cameras registered and anyone taking snapshots without permission will have the film, camera, or both confiscated.

Finally, while there are many other points that could be covered under etiquette I'd like to touch on one more issue—sexuality. Because our community has unique lifestyles, it's good to consider the comfort of others in regard to public displays, especially when there are young children around. Note, this is a matter of practicality—children may speak of what they see to teachers or friends, and then suddenly all manner of trouble can erupt. This is especially true at clothing-optional sites. The rule of "harm none" means taking precautions that keep you and your family safe too!

A lot of Pagans may seem sexually flirtatious because they're not as worried about physical matters. This does not, however, equate to an open invitation or an atmosphere of a free-for-all. Sexual responsibility is a very important topic discussed regularly in our community. Be honest, be polite, ask questions where you feel the need, and remember that perfect love and perfect trust does not equal sex. In fact, it means honoring our physicality (in all its diversity) in ways that are respectful and free of assumptions. The more we release each other from unrealistic or worldly expectations, the more we will see each other as Sacred Beings. If we allow all our actions, interactions, and reactions to flow from that starting point, we'll be doing well indeed.

Fairies

Don't ask questions of fairy tales.   —JEWISH PROVERB

Witches are aware that the world we experience with our senses is only part of a much larger picture—a picture that includes other realms, energies, and beings. Fairies in particular are a type of devic being that attaches itself to a specific element or realm. Some take notice of humans because of a particular personality or awareness they possess (especially spiritual sensitivity). Thus witches sometimes find their lives filled with unexpected and unseen guests.

The names for such entities change depending on culture, but global myths and legends are filled with them. Armenians call them the *dey*, Persians call them *daeva*, the Malaysians believe in the *Chinoi*, Algonquians the *manitu*, Japanese speak of *Marishi-ten*, and Tibetans the *sa-bdag*. The characteristics and living places for such creatures vary, but in nearly all settings there are spells and charms to either encourage the being's assistance, to enable one to see and interact with the beings, or those who protect you from their mischief.

Of course European lore contributed much to our current conception of these beings, but for the purpose of this section, I'll focus on the "shining ones" described in the Vedas as that seems to be where the concept of the fairy folk originated. It's thought that these creatures are somewhat like demigods in that they are a force of nature that motivates life from outside (the astral) in (the temporal). In this way, the fairies give the phrase "out of space, out of time" a whole new meaning as they interact both with the here and the not-here equally well. They are, in fact, a transmitting source that helps connect the energy patterns of all things in all dimensions.

When such beings decide to make their presence known in your life, it's typically through odd events—items moved around or missing, dislocated sounds, wafting aromas, etc. When things like this start happening, you can try to discover the source magickally. Here are some of the items witches have traditionally used to locate, see, or, if necessary, safeguard themselves from the fairy folk:

- *Silver:* Irish people carried a silver knife to keep mischievous fairies at bay.

- *Four-leaf clover:* Lay some grains of wheat on this to open the fairy world to your eyes.

- *Hazel:* Make a divining rod from this wood and search out any hidden or unseen beings.

- *Gourd:* Leave a gourd outside your door as a ward against fairy glamoury (if you can find one that has a reddish hue, all the better).

- *Oak, ash, and thorn:* A sacred triad of trees where fairies gather.

- *Peony:* A special children's amulet to safeguard them from the fey.

- *Primrose:* When planted in your garden, primrose will attract fairies.

- *Straw:* Some believe fairies make their homes here.

- *Thyme:* Wear a sprig to open the unseen world to you.

We should always be aware that elemental beings like fairies may have wholly different agendas than our own, and do not always appreciate human dabbling. I generally recommend caution when interacting with the elementals and fairies and treating them with all due respect.

Fear and Courage

> *Whatever you do, you need courage. Whatever course you decide upon, there is always someone to tell you that you are wrong. There are always difficulties arising that tempt you to believe your critics are right. To map out a course of action and follow it to an end requires some of the same courage that a soldier needs. Peace has its victories, but it takes brave men and women to win them.* —RALPH WALDO EMERSON

A lot of people misunderstand fear. In some languages the word translates more like "respect." This makes sense. Take for example the fear of fire. From a purely pragmatic viewpoint this is actually respect for that element, knowing full well if we abuse it we'll get burned. So Granny would like you to consider that some "fears" are healthy—they keep us from doing stupid things. They act like the yellow light saying "slow down, do you really want to do this?" Listen to such voices long enough to really consider your actions or words.

Other fears are not healthy because they overwhelm us, sometimes to the point of finding ourselves completely unable to function. Some of those fears seem to have no real source that you can pinpoint. To illustrate: I've been afraid of spiders all my life but nothing happened to me as a child (of which I'm consciously aware) that would cause that fear. This type of fright is something on which one can work, slowly and diligently, to at least understand and overcome. For me, I suspect the spider fear ties into the "creepy crawlies"—those images that because they're not "beautiful" get equated with darkness and other icky things. Yeah, I know—not very scientific, but honest. In understanding your fears and coping with them, honesty with yourself is very important. That's one huge key to successfully overcoming the problem.

Honesty and mindfulness also come to bear in working on the fears that you understand. For example, I almost fell out of a roller coaster when I was young, so I'm terrified of ever going back on one. And in fact, I probably never will simply because I see no great need to do so. However, I do not keep my children away from that experience simply because it's a place I choose not to go. That's handling my fear honestly, but also in a mindful way so I don't teach them to be afraid of this situation just because I am!

On the flip side of fear we have courage. Now, before you think that courage is only a positive attribute I should mention that boldness and bravery have negative sides too. How many times have you heard the expression "going where angels fear to tread"? That aphorism came about because when we're really pumped up and all that courage courses through our veins, sometimes reason (the logical self) gets blurred. We jump in and either harm ourselves or others by rash action. So, just as you learn to understand and work with your fears, so, too, should you look at courage with a truthful and mindful eye.

If you're working magick specifically to help bolster courage in a situation where you feel your misgivings may undermine functionality, there are various components, colors, and symbols that may help. In particular red, gold, and orange are hues that support personal resolve, so bring those colors into your wardrobe that day. Carry hematite or beryl in your pocket as a touchstone, and dab on some cedar or thyme oil as a subtle aromatic cue. In terms of symbols, look for a small lion carving to give you that brave heart. Be it colors, stones, or symbols, however, don't forget to take the time to bless and energize the components you're using for your magick before putting them to work for you. Perhaps a small blessing like: *Fear has no place in me, turn away, turn away. Only courage may stay, I claim my power here, today!*

Another good option for this type of magick is utilizing knots (see later in this book). Take a strand of red yarn and put eight knots in it (for firm foundations and confidence). You can use the same invocation as with the previous blessing. Carry this with you, untying one knot when you feel your resolve waning. Note however that the last knot should never be undone, since this dissolves the spell. When you get to the last knot, recharge the strand, and add new knots to it to equal eight once more.

Feng Shui

Just as your car runs more smoothly and requires less energy to go faster and farther when the wheels are in perfect alignment, you perform better when your thoughts, feelings, emotions, goals, and values are in balance.
—BRIAN TRACY

Feng Shui, or the art of placement, comes to us from the Far East. In this system everything from single objects to whole homes are thoughtfully placed to inspire (or re-establish balance in) the positive flow of energy (called *chi*). This *chi* energy is already a part of all things, and as we recognize it and begin to direct it effectively, it in turn promotes wholeness in body, mind, and spirit.

Granny has found that many global methods work wonderfully as an adjunct to magick. Feng Shui is one such approach, especially in terms of where you place charms, amulets, and other sacred objects in your home. To understand this and use it successfully, you'll need to first review the correspondences for each direction of a space, room, or home.

North: This region rules over our jobs and careers. The traditional colors that support this energy are blue and black. The element for North is water (as opposed to the Wiccan Earth association). When you find you're having issues with coworkers, when you're thinking about a career change, when you want advancement, or when you need to restore balance between your personal life and business, this is the best region in which to work magick (or to place a charm or other sacred item that represents your goal). For example, in keeping with the colors and element here you might place a small fountain that contains prosperity-oriented stones near the northern part of your office to encourage not only success but financial stability.

It's important to look closely at this region when career trouble arises. If, for example, a layoff may be imminent, and the northern region of your work or personal space is highly cluttered—clean it! Put everything in order and find some blue or black items to restore the *chi* in that region. In particular, light a blue candle here with the intention of being at peace with the situation, and trusting for the best possible outcome.

Northeast: This region rules over matters of the conscious mind, particularly learning. Its colors are yellow and brown, and its element is earth. We need our logical, rational selves to keep one foot on the ground. When you find you're daydreaming too much, and need to reconnect with terra firma, meditate in this part of your room or home and then don some yellow or brown clothing to keep those foundations with you throughout the day.

As one might expect the northeast is the best space in any room in which to study. If you can set a potted plant nearby (for growing awareness), all the better. Also, during those times when you find your mind filled with distracting unanswered questions, issues, etc., consider lighting a yellow candle here and let all that mental clutter melt away in its flame.

East: East belongs to your family and health matters. It's also the place of new beginnings. The colors here should be light blue and bright green. The element is wood. This is the direction that has the most direct correlation to Wiccan symbolism.

When you're having trouble getting started on something new, light a sky-blue or shoot-green candle here. Keep your intention clearly in mind. In this case, the flame literally represents putting a fire under that new project or goal!

If you find that you or your family have been plagued with ongoing colds and flu, check this region of your home. If there are closed curtains or doorways—open them up to release that negative energy. If there's lots of clutter, put things away so the *chi* can flow, then follow with a good, old-fashioned smudging with sage or cedar to renew the healthful magick.

Southeast: The focus of the southeast is on overall abundance and creativity. The traditional colors are dark blues and greens, and the element is wood. We're beginning to get closer to sun-oriented energy here, which brings blessings with each drop of light.

If you'd like to encourage prosperity, find a wooden plant holder and place in it something that blossoms. Magickally speaking basil, dill, chamomile, or mint are all good choices since they already bear the appropriate energy pattern. You might also consider putting a green stone, like a moss agate, in the bottom, which not only promotes plant growth but is of the right hue to support your financial goals.

For artists of any type who find they're facing creative blockages, move your working area to this region. If that's not practical, at least you can light a green candle here to help get your creative energies back on track.

South: Southern energies encourage honor, acceptance, and power. The colors here are vibrant red and purple, and the element is fire. Because of all the power of light this region holds, it shines on everything you do. Thus, this part of a house or room often speaks of how other people perceive you or your work. For example, if everything here is very open and airy, those around you may consider you very open-minded, especially to new ideas.

Work magick here to help get rid of old, outmoded expectations that others may have toward you (or images that you've long since outgrown). Also consider placing an incense burner in this part of your home to honor the fire element. Light some mint incense here when you wish to be welcome and accepted in another's home (it encourages hospitality) or ginger incense when you want to improve your overall energy reserves.

Southwest: This region rules over our relationships and sense of happiness. The colors here should be brown and yellow, and the element is Earth. The overall luck, love, harmony, and understanding of your household members resides in this region—so don't neglect it! In particular make sure this part of your space or home isn't blocked off, or you may find that you likewise close your heart to love.

Whenever a new friend or animal comes into your life, this is an excellent space in which to celebrate that connection. Light a brown candle dabbed with an earthy incense (like patchouli) as a way of saying thank you to Spirit. This, in turn, also helps foster the growth of your relationship with Spirit.

West: The West belongs to your children, specifically their luck and future. The colors here are white, silver, and gold, and the element is metal. For those without physical children, bear in mind that "children" can be taken metaphorically to mean pets, personal projects, your arts, or even a business that has become like a child to your mind and heart. It may also have to do with an actual child that you feel fondly toward (perhaps the son or daughter of a friend who just adores you too). In any case, work your magick in this region when any of these literal or figurative children seem to be ailing, or when you wish to give them the gift of positive energy by way of blessings.

Northwest: The northwest presides over those helpful people in your life, and anything pertaining to service and networking. The colors are white, silver, and gold, and the element is metal.

When you need to give of your time and efforts to a group, build up your energy in this space beforehand so it's truly service given with a smile (the best kind of service in my opinion). If you find you're having trouble giving or receiving help, this region may be blocked in some way—take a look around and find out how to open both it and your heart again!

Consider finding a special metal candle holder with a white, silver, or gold candle to leave in this region. When you find that you need assistance from others for anything, light the candle to get that positive energy burning brightly. And don't forget to reach out! *Chi* cannot help you if you don't open those doors in your life so it can flow to where it's most needed.

As an aside, if anyone reading this wishes to set up a special altar for your family, friends, teachers—anyone you wish to honor—the northwest is the place to put it. It's a fantastic way to show respect for those who have helped us on our path, and a means by which we can say "thank you" spiritually.

What exactly can you expect from blending Feng Shui with magick? Mostly gentle, slow changes. Many people live out of balance all their lives. Even a few years where your *chi* has been maladjusted will take time to repair. Additionally, long lasting transformation often takes time, persistence, and ongoing maintenance. You won't find quick fixes here, just a helpmate.

Remember that Feng Shui isn't just about the external actions, it's about the internal process those actions represent. Our bodies are the figurative "room" for our spirits, so the truest and best work must begin within. Get rid of the clutter in your mind and heart. Release that which you no longer need, or those things that aren't healthy. Clean up your spirit, and light the candle that is your soul. As you do this, you'll naturally find that everything improves both mundanely and magickally.

Fertility

The management of fertility is one of the most important functions of adulthood. —GERMAINE GREER

Before going any further, Granny should mention that "fertility" need not pertain only to humans. Throughout history fertility magick has been used for everything from improving birthing among farm animals to the yield in a field. In a modern setting it might also apply to abundant job leads, fertile gardens, or even a productive imagination! So don't limit yourself in the way you apply fertility charms, spells, potions and other mystical methods.

Fertility seems closely tied with the air element and the colors of yellow or sprout green (indicating new growth). It's also associated with dawn (a new beginning) and the season of spring (when the earth shows signs of fertility). You can keep those basic associations in mind when creating your own fertility magicks.

To that foundation you can add any of these components:

- *Amber:* Images of fish or frogs when carried are said to ensure conception (note that if applying the amber to something other than physical fertility this image should be placed accordingly, such as among the seeds of your garden).

- *Geodes:* A natural womb symbol, these are said to protect against miscarriage.

- *Pearls:* Wear to inspire fertility.

- *Barley:* The Greeks mixed this with beer to improve fertility, while in China carrying it improves potency.

- *Bread:* The symbolic value of "rising" is the key here. Add an herb to your bread that represents the area of your life in which you desire fertility, then internalize the magick by eating.

- *Dates or figs:* A common component in fertility fare.

- *Berries:* A strong symbol due to their abundance.

- *Pomegranates:* Featured in Babylonian and Asian weddings to ensure the couple's fertility.

- *Nuts:* Sacred to many different deities, nuts resemble male procreative parts and therefore (using the law of similars) were used for fertility spells. Banana has similar connotations.

Putting all this information together isn't too difficult. You can make yourself date-nut bread for physical fertility, or carry nuts with your artistic tools to provide you with abundant ideas. Sprinkle barley to the winds with your fertile wishes, or tuck an image of the area of your life needing fertility into a geode.

Festivals, Holidays, and Celebrations

I once wanted to become an atheist, but I gave up—they have no holidays.
                                                        —HENNY YOUNGMAN

Around the world, right now, people are celebrating. Some gather to honor a God or Goddess, some the birth of a child, others the anniversary of an important cultural event, and others still to commemorate the season. No matter the reason, festivals and celebrations are one of the ways humans create an annual rhythm—a construct that draws those of similar backgrounds or ideals together regularly. In a highly mobile society, this may be among the most important things witches continue to do as part of our tradition (even solitary practitioners who get together with others at open circles).

In a book of this nature, rather than talking so much about the wheel of the year and various specific magickal celebrations that have been done to death, I'd like to focus a little more on the human element—the whys of celebration and what it does for our soul. See, that part of the picture is often missing. We become so accustomed to going through the motions that the meaning of what we're doing often gets lost. That's a terrible pity, and something each one of us can change.

I already mentioned that celebrations provide a cyclical beat of sorts—one that we mark on calendars and with best laid plans. That continuity and familiarity is important, as is honoring tradition. But what else do festivals provide? For one thing, celebrations encourage fellowship, especially for those who practice most of their magick alone. For another thing, celebrating gives us an all-important moment to pause and consider all that came before this moment, and all that's about to be. That moment is precious for internalization and meaningful comprehension. After all, if we're just enacting our rites like a droning dogma, there's no real power there. In fact, I'd say it was a complete waste of time.

Meaningful Moments

So how exactly do we keep ourselves from getting too caught up in approaching celebrations by rote, and instead really making them sing with meaning for everyone gathered? In answer to that question, I've put together some good questions and things to think about:

- Did your family mark this holiday or celebration in any manner? If so, was there something special you can translate into your magick?

- Is there any cultural (family line) significance to this celebration and if so can you consider adding cultural touches to round out the sensual input?

- Beyond the traditional correspondences for this celebration— ask yourself what it means to *you* and what's happening in your life right now. How can you honor that spiritually?

- What type of special preparations can you make to encourage a deeper appreciation of the energies? Examples here include fasting for a day before the ritual (if physically feasible) or foregoing something that normally distracts you from spiritual matters (like TV) for a set amount of time.

- What sensual cues can you bring to the celebration to improve the overall impact for yourself or others? Think sights, symbols, aromas, clothing (costume), decorations, postritual foods... the whole shebang!

- How can you share meaningfulness with others? Typically, allowing them a voice in the preparations helps a lot—the more that participants get involved, usually the more excitement occurs. Excitement = energy!

- Don't be afraid to observe "old" traditions in whole new ways.

Breathe a little fresh air into your observances (consider this getting bonus points for creativity).

Finally, when you cannot go to a celebration or observance because of personal constraints, either find a way to honor that moment in your own home, or adapt that celebration to another global observance for which you do have time. For example, say you have to work on Halloween. Since this is the Celtic New Year, look to the timing of other global New Year's celebrations instead. Adapt the ideas, symbols, and customs from those festivals gently into your own observance, and generate all the same energies! If you always remember that magick works outside time and space, the timing is really a moot point. What's most important is taking that pause to breathe, to understand, to rejoice, and to *be*.

Finding Lost Items

There is no shame in not knowing; the shame lies in not finding out.
—RUSSIAN PROVERB

I hate it when I lose things. I will spend hours searching wildly for something only to discover, usually after I give up, that it was right in front of me all along (or perhaps a playful fairy was helping out!). Then I realized that this is the type of situation for which magick is a perfect helpmate. Since magick works with the "unseen" realm, its energy is well suited to uncovering such things.

Typically I use one of two approaches. The first is an adaptation on knot and string magick. Take an item that represents what you lost (or a piece of paper on which you've written a description of the item). Wrap this around thrice with string, leaving enough extra to place the packet across from you on your altar or tabletop.

Now, visualize this item. Bring it clearly into your mind, but as if you're viewing it remotely (which you are). Begin to gather the string slowly into your hand continually saying "return to me." As the packet on the table comes closer to you, change the mental image so that it, too, appears closer. When the bundle reaches your hand, your visualization should be that of the item being back in your hands. Keep that bundle in a safe place until that item, or a replacement, manifests itself.

The second approach is dowsing. This is most effective if you have a pretty good idea of the area in which you lost the item. Take your dowsing rod (if you don't have one—look for a Y-shaped stick. The two ends of the Y are held in your hands with the main branch forward). Begin walking the land with the main branch parallel to the ground. As with the string spell, keep a strong image in your mind of the item. When you begin getting closer the twig will start twitching or feeling as if it's pulled downward. Look in that area closely. Sometimes this process marks a region within which the object lies (by marking a circle of "hits"—the term used for the end of the twig moving down sharply to the earth). Other times it comes very close to, or on top of, the object.

By the way, it's interesting to note that "water witching" (dowsing) was highly regarded up to 100 years ago. So much was the case that the Department of the Interior had a report compiled on the history and successful use of dowsing rods. This study was led by the director of the United States Geological Survey, Mr. George Otis Smith, and presented in 1917.

Fire Magick

We should take from the past its fires and not its ashes.

—JEAN JAURÈS

Fire was undoubtedly the most significant element to our ancestors. The sun's fire provided light and warmth, as did the tribal fire at night. The discovery of fire forever changed humankind's fate in this world. So it's not surprising to hear Shamans tell us that fire is very powerful. It is also the most difficult element with which to work spiritually.

Like a sword, the element of fire has two very different sides—one is warm and illuminating, the other is furious and burning. These are neither "good" nor "bad" in and of themselves. It's simply fire's way. It cannot help be what it is in energies and patterns. Thus, when we talk about fire magick we do so cautiously and respectfully, knowing that it can empower, enlighten, and comfort as surely as it can destroy if allowed to get out of hand.

With that bit of caution out of the way, let's take a look at how to utilize fire energy in our magick safely. First, fire represents the heart and hearth. It is around a fire that our ancestors gathered to share food and maintain community ties. I find it no small coincidence that modern neo-Pagan gatherings always feature a community fire where attendees can dance to the sound of drums, sing, and engage in fellowship. This is an excellent use of fire! Many fire keepers tell me that they try to use natural lighting supplies so that the spiraling energy isn't hindered by chemicals, so you may wish to consider that option when building your own. If someone else has built the fire, however, please honor that person's duty and responsibility. Don't go poking in the fire without permission. This is part of respecting the element as well as each other in the sacred space.

In terms of utilizing small or large fires specifically for magickal goals, the easiest way to do so is by placing herbs or other natural items therein to burn. Such things should be chosen to represent your goal.

Then as the smoke moves out from that point, it carries your wishes with it.

Another way to use the fire's warmth is by placing an item or object that symbolizes someone or something to which you wish to bring more energy (literally "warming it up"). I've found this particularly effective when it comes to emotional matters (including when I'm feeling rather coldhearted). Note that if you can't have an actual fire, another figurative fire source will do, like a household heater, the stove, or even a hair dryer!

Candles or other enclosed fire sources offer us other ways to utilize fire's energy. Candles show up in so many types of magick that it's nearly impossible to mention all of the applications (see also *Candles*). The flame of the candle represents the light of our spirit or the Divine. As it burns, our energy is directed outward toward manifestation.

And what about the remnants from fire—namely ashes? Well, these can become part of power pouches and portable altars. Sprinkling the ashes from a sacred fire around an area is one way to bless it. Carrying those ashes likewise transports the energy of the fire (and the fire's purpose) with you. In particular Granny likes to have a pinch of ash from festival fires so that I can feel closer to my long-distance family until we gather again.

In brief, fire magick is best utilized for goals such as:

- Improving the happiness and compassion in any relationship

- Discovering the truth or hidden things (coming out of the shadows)

- Increasing personal energy

- Banishing negative thoughts, habits, or vibrations

- Illuminating the path toward transformation

- Kick-starting passion for anyone or anything

- Motivating improved self image (the light of awareness and confidence)

- Generating strength or victory

- Inspiring comprehension on a deeply meaningful level

As with any magick fire is but a tool. You are still the enabler. Please be careful and wise. Let your fires burn slowly, and tend them well so that they don't go out, nor spark something that you did not intend.

Focus

No life ever grows great until it is focused, dedicated, disciplined.
—Harry Emerson Fosdick

It would surprise me greatly to attend any class on magick, or read any good book on spirituality that did not include information on the importance of focus. Magickally speaking focus means two things—it means our personal awareness (those things to which we give heed) *or* it means an item or object through which we direct our will. In the case of the latter the focus is intended to amplify and guide the energies.

Let's go a little further, however. If focus encompasses our personal awareness, then it also embraces how we view things. Consider the phrase "watch and learn" as a starting point in this process. We must *watch* to *learn*, but the process of focus—of observation—is not done simply with our eyes; all our senses should participate, including magickal ones. Why am I stressing this? Because I believe that if a person cannot learn to see beyond the superficial into the potentialities of life, his or her spiritual life will be very, very limited. Additionally I believe that there are times when we allow our focus and attention to remain in all the wrong places—in negativity, in past failures, in the proverbial *would-should-could-haves* of our life. When this happens we miss wonderful moments and opportunities that are right before us.

Open a New View

Getting past preconceived notions or unhealthy focal points isn't easy. We have to train our minds to think differently, and then apply that new perspective in how we focus our attention and will. There is a process that you can follow, however, that will help you determine if your focus is healthy and if you're activating it effectively. Begin by simply being willing to ask yourself if you're sure. Assurance is something you can feel deep in your soul like an anchor. If that center isn't there—something's amiss.

Second, ask yourself what you're doing right here, and right now. Be mindful of this moment. The past is not now. The future is not now. And when you're working magick, there is neither time nor space about which to worry! All time is *now*. Don't miss the moment.

Third, consider if you're repeating a positive pattern or a negative habit. Not all minirituals in life (our routines, dispositions, mannerisms) are good for us; not all of the things that grab our focus are good for us. And since, spiritually speaking, like attracts like—it's always good to know what kind of patterns you're attracting, and hopefully why, too!

Finally, slowly but surely, begin repatterning. Weed out those fears, angers, and insecurities, and replace them with confidence, peace, and love. The person whose ultimate focus is cultivating love in its purest form is also one who works for the good of All. Perfect love does not allow you to manipulate, and it need not see the world through rose-colored glasses. If we have the love of Spirit in our lives, we see clearly, we think clearly, and then we put thought and will into action in our magick.

Now, before you feel overwhelmed by this task (it's no small challenge) be aware that adjusting your focus to not only global but universal truths and energies takes time, patience, and fortitude. You won't get there overnight. Sometimes we don't get there in several lifetimes! But this concept illustrates a saying that I've often shared with my students: *Keep your eyes on the horizon, but know well the road on which you walk.* If we're always looking up, we're likely to fall into a pothole. If we're always looking down, we forget where we're going and why. When our focus is in balance, however, it helps everything in our life flow better—including our ability to direct our will in magick.

Forgiveness

Forgiveness does not mean ignoring what has been done or putting a false label on an evil act. It means, rather, that the evil act no longer remains as a barrier to the relationship. —MARTIN LUTHER KING, JR.

To err is human. Everyone falls on his or her nose from time to time. The question becomes what do we do about it—not just the person who erred, but also those affected by that error? Our ancestors often resorted to curses at such time, but typically for something considered a truly nasty offense (or as the result of the anger of the moment). Modern witches who feel that the karmic boomerang isn't welcome, however, may want to consider another approach.

Now, Granny is not going to tell you "live and let live" is the right perspective 100 percent of the time. That outlook, while it has good points, doesn't always balance out any resulting harm in the equation. When we err, we need to *fix it.* And if we fix it, those who were harmed will hopefully forgive us so that everyone can move forward. Bear in mind that I'm talking about people who sincerely want to make things right—not those who are simply looking for a convenient "out" by saying "I'm sorry" (and then typically go on to do the very same thing again).

Basically I don't want well-meaning, good-hearted neo-Pagans to become doormats for the users of the world. On the other hand, I don't want them to miss out on valuable opportunities to heal, either. When you're working on the latter, here's one miniritual to try when your body and mind are willing to accept the binding tie of Spirit in the process.

Reconnect

Hurt or harm causes disconnection in varying degrees. Fitting the energies of disconnected people back together into the pattern of wholeness isn't always easy. I see those energies as the strands we send out— the binding ties (if you will) that create a tapestry. Each person's tapestry is different. Each strand attaches itself to different places, people, and things. Typically we don't get angry at a place or a thing, so this particular activity is directed toward people who need to mend their relationship and reconnect.

If it is possible to have the other individual(s) involved in the situation present for the miniritual it really helps. The sacred space (a circle) puts us all back into equality. Here no one person is greater or less than another. It is in that spirit that the sacred space should be set using an invocation that shares the intention. For example:

> *Guardian of the East, breathe on us with the winds of a fresh beginning*
> *Guardian of the South, burn away our anger and illuminate the darkness of hidden*
> *   resentments*
> *Guardian of the West, wash away the old and begin to heal our hearts*
> *Guardian of the North, enrich our desire to grow and learn from this*
> *And to leave the past behind*

From here the ritual can take one of two forms. The first uses seeds. Put a bowl of any type of birdseed on the table. Each person in turn takes a small pinch of seeds and voices the last of their pain, sorrow, or anger in honesty. That then goes into another empty bowl. When everyone is done, they take hold of the bowl together and throw it out to the winds so that the anger disperses and something good grows in its place.

The second form is what I call web weaving. Each person should bring a long strand of yarn (one for each participant) that represents himself or herself. Then each person braids his or her strand of yarn into the strands of others present, one at a time. As the strands cross, place therein wishes for healing, joy, and peace. Cut the braid into as many equal segments as there are contributors: Everyone take home one piece to keep safe as a reminder of the commitment you have made.

Obviously a forgiveness ritual isn't really an ending. It's a beginning, and one to which everyone must give ongoing energy for it to find fulfillment and manifestation. If you're not wholly committed to putting the past behind and healing broken bonds, don't participate. Truth to self requires that we know what steps we're ready to take and when. Just don't hold on too tightly to anger or bitterness. Grieve, feel, *be* . . . then find a way to move forward from that space into something better.

Fortunetelling

*The whole world is an omen and a sign. Why look so wistfully in a cor-
ner? Man is the Image of God. Why run after a ghost or a dream? The
voice of divination resounds everywhere and runs to waste unheard, un-
regarded, as the mountains echo with the bleatings of cattle.*
                                                    —Ralph Waldo Emerson

Be it understanding the here and now, or looking toward tomorrow,
there are few of us who couldn't use a little more insight. Every person
has spiritual vision to some degree. It's just a matter of learning how to
open those figurative eyes! This section gives you helpful hints on doing
just that, and also shares some easy to use divination systems that can
be found right around the house!

First you should know that a psychic nature is natural. We all have
instincts; it's just that some are more developed than others. It might
take you a while to get good at divination readings because, like exercis-
ing a new muscle, practice makes perfect. When you first start trying,
please be patient with yourself.

For novices and "old pros" alike my key advice is to keep track of
your readings diligently and encourage anyone who gets a reading from
you to likewise take notes. I can't tell you how many times people have
come back to me wishing they'd been a little more attentive because
something in the reading was now starting to make sense. See, because
our senses are working outside of time, it can be days, weeks, months,
and sometimes years before the results from a reading become clear to
us in the mundane world. Better still, readings can take on whole new
meanings over time, and still prove just as insightful. But having notes
or tapes to refer to builds confidence in yourself, or your chosen reader.
That confidence fuels improved reliability.

Helps and Hints

For those who seem to have trouble with divination there are a few things that may help.

1. First, in choosing a system pick the one that really appeals to your senses. If you're a highly visual person, for example, tarot or other cards might prove much more appealing and offer more input than runes, which have less symbolism and a more tactile nature.

2. Second, try to release any expectations of what type of information you're likely to get from a reading. In other words don't go looking for information in the reading that isn't there. Why? While most people pose a specific question, Spirit sometimes has more pressing matters to communicate! Thus it's totally possible to get answers to a question that wasn't asked, or information regarding a situation that you hadn't fully considered before the reading. Do not take such readings as "failures"— they're huge successes!

3. Third, give any new divination system a fair chance. I typically suggest working with it for at least three to six months, during which time you study the symbols and try various layouts, castings, or whatever. By the end of that time frame you'll have accomplished three things. You'll understand this system more intimately, you'll have developed your own inner sight, and you'll have determined whether this particular method will work effectively and consistently for you. If not, try another, and keep trying till you find a system that works or you find a friend who is adept in divination and to whom you can turn.

4. Fourth, always avoid reading for yourself or others when you're ill, angry, or otherwise out of sorts. Also don't read if you feel

you cannot put aside personal prejudice or feelings regarding a situation or person involved in the reading to see what's really there. Such feelings typically taint a reading.

Last of all, recognize that divination won't answer all of life's questions. Use it when you need additional perspective, but don't run to it twenty times over the same issue. I cannot tell you how many times people go to a reader hoping to hear what they *want* to hear instead of what they *need* to hear. The phrase "Yes, other readers have told me that" comes up in sessions all the time, to which I reply "So why haven't you *done* it?" Just like any metaphysical method, one should be ready to follow up what you learn through divination with substantive action in the mundane world so a positive manifestation will occur.

Modern Adaptive Methods

Now, Granny knows a lot of folks are on tight budgets. She also recognizes that there's nothing wrong with a little creativity. I've looked in and around my house and found the following items that could be used for a personalized divination system in which you assign the meanings to each piece:

- Colored buttons (interpret by size and/or shape).

- Dry beans (cast various colored ones onto a paper surface and scry the results).

- Anything in your junk drawer (reach in blindly with a question in mind and pull out an answer).

- Alphabet soup (scry the surface).

- Weeds: Go outside, sit down, think of a question, and randomly pull up the first plant that comes into your hand. Interpret according to prevalent plant/herb symbolism (this works in flower gardens too).

- Clouds: Scry the patterns while lying lazily on the grass and thinking of a question.

- Nuts, bolts, nails, etc. (make a good caste system).

- Books: Grab one randomly and interpret either a title or a spot of text on which your eyes immediately fall.

- Greeting cards or coupons: use the words on the cards or coupons, or the imagery, for interpretive value.

I'm sure if you look around your home you'll find even more potential divination tools. It just takes considering the most mundane of items as having the potential for spiritual and magickal possibilities.

Freedom *(Liberation)*

Nowhere does a man retire with more quiet or freedom than into his own soul. ——MARCUS AURELIUS

If you ever find yourself feeling trapped or constrained by circumstances, expectations, the past, prejudices, or habits, then you're not alone. Freedom—in body, mind, and spirit—is important to most people and especially to those walking alternative spiritual Paths. So how do we overcome those things that bind or constrict in an unhealthy way?

In part, Granny says that old-fashioned elbow grease is a good place to begin. We have the power to make and change our lives if we're willing to apply a four-letter word: WORK. Even with a willingness to be diligent, however, some things take more than just honest effort to change. That's when and where you look to your magick for aid.

Because freedom and liberation take a variety of different forms depending on your focus, I'd like to walk you through a good process for finding the best symbols and components for spells, meditations, and rituals.

Finding Focal Points and Symbols for Freedom

1. To what part of your life does this issue pertain? Write down several words on a piece of paper describing that part of your life or issue.

2. From step one, make a list of any symbols, tokens, or objects that you associate with the core problem. For example, if you're trying to liberate yourself from smoking, cigarettes and matches might be the symbols or tokens. If you're trying to liberate yourself from a group of people who aren't life affirming, you might gather poppets or dolls to represent those individuals.

3. Now choose something to represent your bondage. A lot of people find yarn, string, rubber bands, paper clips, tape, or other types of adhesives a good choice since the mind already associates these things with connection.

4. Also pick a symbol of liberation. Butterflies are one that's nearly universal, but what you choose *must* be personally significant as this is what you want to claim at the end of the process.

5. Place the symbol of bondage around the token you've chosen before you begin your chosen magickal process (note that if you need to represent yourself it's better to use some that you've worn or handled a lot).

6. During your meditation, spell, or ritual, make sure to release the token from the bondage, and then somehow put away or

destroy both the bondage material and the item that represents what you're trying to overcome.

7. At the end of the process, take whatever represents your liberation and claim it! Attach it to your symbol of self or carry it with you until the situation transforms.

This is obviously a very loose overview, but it's one I have found works in nearly all situations if you take the time to think through the process and symbols. The only variation that you may encounter is in visualizations where all the items or objects exist in the arena of your mind only (unless you want to give them a physical representation too).

Gardening

The trouble with gardening is that it does not remain an avocation. It becomes an obsession. —Phyllis McGinley

My husband would agree very heartily with Ms. McGinley's observation. Our yard started with a small vegetable garden and slowly transformed into an ongoing landscaping project! There is just something therapeutic about working closely with the Earth, and helping things grow. I have found it not only very healthy, but also a great way to meditate and reconnect.

For this particular topic, Granny would like to share some nifty magickal gardening tips for both indoor and outdoor gardeners.

Glorious Gardens: Helps and Hints

- Keep a moss agate in your pocket or put a few small ones in your plant's soil. This stone is reputed to be a gardener's ally. Alternative stones include a bloodstone to improve your harvest, coral to keep insects away, and jade to support the overall health of your plants.

- Work growth- or abundance-oriented magicks in or near your garden so they benefit from the energy overflow

- Skip clockwise around your garden, sprinkling it with water as you move. The upward movement of skipping is considered a sympathetic magick that encourages the plants to grow upward.

- Plant lettuce or marjoram in your gardens to protect them, peony to safeguard against storm damage, and sunflowers to generate antibug energies.

- Bless your soil using a libation of cider. This is a very ancient custom. If you want the cider to also deter insects, gently steep some tomato leaves in it, along with other strong aromatics like cedar.

- For flowerpots or windowsill gardens find crystal beads or points that you can hang above the holders. This way the plants grow toward a specific type of energy and are continually saturated with it. Just make sure to match the crystal(s) to the plant's purpose in your magick. For example, amethyst blends well with lavender, fire agate with sunflowers, citrine with chamomile, aventurine with mint, sunstone with marigolds or daisy, and so forth.

- Meditate with your plants. If you take the time to listen closely, they will often tell you what they need in symbolic form. For example, say you notice some mums looking rather blah. As you meditate with the flowers you discover that your mouth gets dry. That indicates the plants aren't getting enough water (this happens a lot with poorly potted plants that you buy at outlets because they're often root bound or the soil loses water too quickly). Or, if you were to suddenly feel as if the air was filled with moisture, check your plant's drainage. They may be drowning. Learning to heed the messages from plant spirits takes some time and practice, so be patient with yourself and them.

- Like any new relationship, you have to learn to speak each other's language!

For those of you who feel like you have a black thumb, I think you'll find that these ideas help a lot. Also, I suggest trying a form of gardening you have not done before. I found I was a dismal indoor gardener but great at outdoor work (the reasons turned out to be very simple—animals and lighting issues). Similarly some people just have a knack for small efforts as opposed to redecorating the entire yard! And don't forget alternatives like hydroponics, water gardens, air gardens, etc. It may take a few tries, but nearly everyone can eventually find a form of gardening that works well with their schedules, space, and magickal goals.

Ghosts

Ghosts seem harder to please than we are; it is as though they haunted for
haunting's sake—much as we relive, brood, and smolder over our pasts.
—Elizabeth Bowen

Beings and powers that normally "hang out" in the etheric realm periodically make their way through the veil between worlds. This experience is difficult for most humans to grasp, simply because our mind has few ways to interpret noncorporeal information. Nonetheless, it seems as if those walking spiritual paths have more encounters of this nature (perhaps because we're open to the experience, and to the concept that there's more to this world than meets the eye).

If you've had odd experiences with "things that go bump" and want to know more, Granny has a treasure trove of lore on ghosts, spirits, hauntings, and the magic that can either draw, banish, or protect you from these entities. Now, some of you may ask why you would ever want to attract a spirit or communicate with it. There are lots of reasons, one being that you have unfinished business with that Being (like a parent or loved one). Another is to try to ascertain the reason for a haunting. Then too, ghosts just make life a little more interesting!

Seeing and Communicating with Spirits

The ancients prescribed a variety of methods for contacting the dead. These included:

- *Conjuration:* Typically formatted for High Magick with appropriate signs and sigils for protection from angry spirits. Midnight seems to be the best time for conjuration, or the hour and day of a person's death.

- Calling upon a spirit during rituals that mark specific turning points (edges) in the year like the New Year, Lammas, and Halloween, during which time the veil between worlds grows thinner.

- *Automatism:* Through writing, pendulums, typing, painting, or dowsing, a spirit can utilize a person's arm to communicate information. Typically a medium, channeler, or sensitive undertakes this process.

- *Channeling and mediumship:* Speaking of channels and mediums, these people allow a spirit to speak through them. This approach is best attempted by someone trained in the art.

- *Ouija:* Something anyone can utilize with proper caution. The Ouija has been dubbed an "open doorway" for spirits, and unless you are specific about to whom you're directing questions and set up proper safeguards to ensure that's who you get, there may be many surprises here!

- *Dreams:* Many people report that they receive messages from spirits while asleep. This is likely due to the fact that our minds are more open and less busy while we rest. However, most often dreams are received from a known entity rather than from a complete stranger.

- *Anointing oil:* Some old books of magick recommend dabbing one's eyelids with a mixture of saffron, aloe, and vervain to improve spiritual sensitivity toward ghosts. I might recommend putting some on your third eye too for the "site."

So, now that you know how to call a ghost, how can you be sure you really have a spiritual guest or haunting? Here are some signs:

Signs of Ghosts or Hauntings

As you examine stories from various people about their encounters with ghosts, it's interesting to note that each person interprets the spirit's presence slightly differently, and very often through a specific sense. Included in this list of telltale signs we find:

- Odd behavior among children and pets (playing with or barking at what appears to our eyes as nothing).

- Aromas whose source cannot be located (often a perfume or cologne worn by the deceased).

- Noises (those proverbial bumps in the night).

- Objects moving: While this seems more common with fairies, ghosts have been known to rearrange pictures and other small items to their liking.

- Elemental oddities, like a fire that burns cold on only one side without any draft present, a wind moving through a house full of closed windows, or cold spots.

- Dreams (discussed above).

- Emotional sensations like sadness or anger when entering a specific area (note that this area must not have any such emotion attached to it for you).

- Visual or physical manifestations, like feeling someone brush by you or seeing light moving through a room.

And what about a spirit that isn't friendly or whose presence is constantly disruptive? How do you solve such problems?

Ghost Remedies

- Name the spirit while tying a string or robe thrice, then bury it outside the house.

- Sprinkle blessed water or anointing oil, or spread the smoke from a smudge stick throughout the house to clear away unwanted energies.

- Scatter dill, fennel, and salt mixed together around the exterior of the room or house.

- Leave basil on the person's grave to ensure the spirit a peaceful afterlife.

- Carry lodestone as an amulet against baleful spirits.

- Pieces of rowan wood, red thread, and seashells are considered strong antighost talismans. Carry them in a power pouch, or leave a bundle near your hearth.

- Grow violets in your garden (apparently malevolent spirits do not like this flower).

- Contact a sensitive and see if the ghost has unfinished business that you may be able to resolve.

- Enact a banishing ritual (take care, however, in that not all spirits go gently into that good night!).

I have had the interesting pleasure of ghosts coming into and out of my life from time to time. I must say it keeps things from getting boring, and I often learn much from the experience.

God/dess (*Spirit*)

The God/dess is alive and magick is afoot.   —THE LORESINGER

Granny has a confession to make. Not only does she have a lot of philosophy and ideology to banter about, but she's also a religious old gal. Some Pagans are pantheists, meaning they believe in numerous gods and goddesses and choose to follow a small smattering of them. I am a bit of an oddball in that I'm a monotheistic witch, who sees many faces to one very large, and somewhat incomprehensible being. I also believe in the phrase "thou art God/dess" in that a small spark, or a divine imprint, exists in each one of us.

Now Granny knows better than to say that's what anyone else should believe. Rather, I'd like to take a moment to talk about the place of the Sacred Parent in a witch's life. Not all witches are religious, after all, nor do they need to be so. But when I look at the world it's impossible for me not to notice the wonderful complexity, and the shadowy pattern of something greater than self, or the Universe. However, I cannot prove this factually—it is a matter of faith.

Now knowing that all magick operates on belief and will, you begin to see how and why I feel Spirit plays a role in my practices. For me, this source is a way to not only support the work I'm doing, but it also helps me with self-improvement. Additionally, by taking on the role of cocreator, something greater than myself guides the energy for the best possible good (the good of All), which is something that (in my humanness) I cannot always grasp.

Calling All God/desses

If you decide you want to work in partnership with Spirit in your magickal Path, I would share one piece of advice. Choose a small assortment (two to four) of Divine figures to call upon regularly, and get to know everything you can about them. Whether you see this being as one or many, honor, respect, and gratitude is very important.

For example, even as a monotheist, I would not randomly call upon one of God's names without having first:

- Researched the energies (characteristics, aptitudes, areas of dominion) in that name
- Understood localized cultural myths about that Being
- Determined appropriate ways to adorn the sacred space for that Being (and done so)
- Confirmed suitable offerings, libations, or traditional prayers

Why go through all that extra trouble? For the same reason that you wouldn't randomly walk up to a stranger's house asking for aid. It's rude (not to mention a bit foolhardy). We must have an understanding of, and appreciation for the energies with which we work otherwise our magick becomes just rote liturgy or careless power mongering, which can result in a huge mess, no matter how good our intentions.

On a similar note, I issue caution in working with Deities from different pantheons in the *same* sacred space. In our stories, many Gods and Goddesses are jealous, and not all play nicely with other Powers. To randomly invoke a wide variety of God/desses into your sacred space is, in my opinion, an open invitation for Chaos herself to visit. This, again, is where knowing your God/desses becomes nothing less than essential. If you've developed a relationship with them, you will know which ones interact positively with others of the same, or different, pantheons.

I realize that may seem like a lot to think about, but it makes for really good food for thought. As we interact with Spirit, the vibrations in our aura shift slightly. The more we welcome Spirit into our lives, the more we can become "thou art God/dess" in word and deed. Therefore, I stand by the idea of "let go and let God/dess" because that means *you* too!

Green Magick

If the sight of the blue skies fills you with joy, if a blade of grass spring-
ing up in the fields has power to move you, if the simple things of nature
have a message that you understand, rejoice, for your soul is alive..."
—ELEONORA DUSE

Green witchery is part of a larger category of metaphysics called Wild Magick. This covers a lot of territory, including druidic practices, Earth mages, hedge witches, shamanic work, and the Cunning Arts (see preface). The thing that connects all these people and concepts is a reverent and protective view of the natural world, as well as an honest appreciation for its potential in our magick.

In looking at green witches in particular, they all seem to have similar ethical, methodical, or philosophical considerations including:

- Safeguarding the Earth's resources

- Honoring the Earth as a Spirit and a sacred living thing

- Developing a rapport with nature's spirits (those of the animal, plant, and mineral kingdom)

- Living in reciprocation with nature (giving back of what we take)

- Nurturing a deep awareness of nature's symbols and lessons (seeing it as a Divine sort of roadmap to the greater pattern in all things)

- Teaching others about nature's patterns and thereby fostering a network of globally minded mages who work on preservation issues

- Respectfully utilizing natural objects and emblems for personal, social, planetary, or universal transformation

These basic concepts are good ones to consider integrating into any positive spiritual Path. Nonetheless, green witchery is considered a specific school of magick, and you might be wondering if it's right for you. The best way to answer that question is to think about how you feel in nature and how you interact with it.

In particular, consider questions like: Do you enjoy long quiet times in any environment where there's no trace of human hands but your own? Do you mind being without all your technical toys (at least for a short haul) or does that leave you feeling apprehensive? Are you perhaps already working extensively with herbs, crystals, animal symbols, etc., and simply didn't have a name for what you were doing?

Answering these types of questions will give you a feel for whether or not you want to venture down this vine-strewn road in the wilderness. And if, indeed, you find your answer is yes, the next step is to get acquainted with the Earth's kingdoms and their powers. In keeping with that idea, Granny recommends any of these books including two and a half that I wrote as good resource material: *Floral Grimoire* and *Herbal Arts* and Scott Cunningham's *Crystal, Gem and Metal Magic,* Paul Beyen's *Herbal Magick* and *Animal Spirit* (by me and Rowan Hall).

Beyond reading, however, it's ultimately important for the green witch to stay in touch with nature and recharge there whenever possible. For those of you living in an urban environment you may find that a neighborhood park, flower conservatory, or nature preserve offers that little getaway you need. Keep spiritually useful plants in and around your home, as the ancient cunning folk did (to keep that natural energy flowing), and remember that even amid the concrete—Earth is just below your feet. Touch her often; handle her with love.

Grounding *(Foundations)*

If you have built castles in the air, your work need not be lost; there is where they should be. Now put foundations under them.

—Henry David Thoreau

Throughout the community there seems to be an ongoing sense of bemusement toward what are termed "fluffy bunny, white light" practitioners. Simply defined, these are the folks who tend to ride a wave of spiritual energy without ever immersing themselves in the water to any real depth. Such individuals have laid no genuine foundations in any spiritual practice—but rather utilize the cultural upswell as a social convention or comfort zone. Granny makes no bones about wanting to take such people aside and give them a good talking to (unfortunately it's usually the media who finds them first!). We need our foundations, and we need to know how to ground to work effective magick.

Before I share some ideas on how to build your foundations and utilize effective grounding methods, I'd like to mention that grounding isn't just effective for putting down roots or channeling off extra energy. It's also a means of attaching a type of energy to a specific area. For example, say you want to have ongoing energy for peace in one room of your house (like the bedroom). You can use various symbols for grounding as a means to connect the peace to that space. In this case, I might actually use a peace symbol attached to the floor or wall with double-sided picture tape to "hold" the energy right where you want it.

Fixing Foundations

With that aside out of the way, let's consider building foundations first. No matter how long you've been on this Path or how adept you may be, the spiritual building process is a lifelong endeavor. Therefore, we need to regularly check and reinforce our foundations to make sure they can hold up over time, and through the daily wear and tear that life causes them. Typically this process requires taking some time, at least once a year, in which you ask yourself some serious questions. For example:

- Do the basics of this Path still motivate you to be the best possible person?

- Do your foundational beliefs continue to challenge you to grow and live out of the box (bearing in mind that magick dies when left to stagnate)?

- Do you find that your beliefs are flexible enough to meet the ongoing changes of the world (especially in terms of scientific knowledge)?

- Have you seen important, ongoing transformations in yourself that you can directly attribute to your Path?

- Do you find joy in the constructs of your beliefs (the rituals, ethics, etc.)?

- Continuing as you are now, can you still see yourself standing firm in this Path in one year's time?

If you answered no to any of these questions, then it's time to seriously consider whether the foundation on which you've built your spirituality needs revision or a complete reconstruction. As we grow and change as people, sometimes that revision/reconstruction becomes necessary and healthy. Don't be afraid of it—welcome it as a way of honoring the new you.

Get a Grip on Grounding

If your foundations are secure, you'll find that learning to ground energy isn't that difficult, unless you have to help someone else do it! There was a lovely young woman who used to visit me all the time, but she was so bouncy that I always felt like I'd had a full pot of coffee when she left. Finally, one day I put my right hand on her heart chakra, my left on her belly, drew a line of energy from there to the floor and said, "Young lady, you're grounded!" The visual and verbal element worked like a charm, and since then I've found it works on pets, children, and me with or without the words. Just remember to draw a silver cord of energy from the person or pet to the earth. It calms them down fairly effectively.

Alternative ways of grounding excess energy include sitting in your yard with your hands palm down so they can channel the vibrations outward to the Earth. Considering the natural force of gravity, Earth is the best grounder for which you could ask! Or, eat some really crunchy veggies (preferably root vegetables) to get those roots back where they belong! Finally, put a small magnet in your shoe so you can always keep one foot on the ground!

Habits

Habits become nature.   —CHINESE PROVERB

Most of the time we hear people talking about bad habits like nail biting or procrastination. Before discussing overcoming such things, however, Granny would like to mention that there are many *good* habits that everyone develops. See, habits are nothing more than a reflection of the patterns in our lives. The way we drive to work, the way we order our kitchens—these are akin to minirituals enacted daily on a very personal level. These rituals (habits) provide an important continuity and familiarity (like comfort food). The only time this is a bad thing is when the pattern proves unhealthy to our body, mind, or spirit.

Change It, Don't Break It

How often have you heard "break the habit" spoken of as if it were a snap? Well, because humans are beings of habit, changing some of those behaviors (especially lifelong ones) is anything but easy. Therefore Granny would like to propose a slightly less daunting solution. Rather than try to break or erase patterns altogether, why not transform them into something positive and functional?

To provide a personal example, I'm a workaholic. It's very hard for me to relax or sit still for any length of time unless I'm ill. So, rather than fight part of what makes me *me*, or even come to hate that aspect of myself, I work with the energy and pour it into specific goals (like completing this book!). While the pattern of overdoing isn't positive, by giving myself set goals, in a defined time frame, I help pace myself and still accomplish something that I can qualify. This is an illustration of what Shamans call repatterning, and you can learn it too.

Repatterning begins with forgiveness. We must allow ourselves room to be human. Bad habits aren't something to hate but rather something from which to learn. Rather than harboring negatives and letting that consume us, we can "swift" the energy for something more positive (to use a friend's word).

Repatterning builds on that forgiveness and then takes the next step, which is determining the source. Ask yourself what situations, people, foods, or whatever lead to the habit you're trying to break. You cannot weed a garden without getting out the roots. Understanding triggers for your habit is a huge step toward victory.

Make a list of those sources and then next to each put down an alternative. For example, my son used to hit his head on the ceiling every time he came up the stairs. The cause here is simply a low ceiling, but the *real* problem was that he was moving too quickly and didn't stop to duck. By isolating the actual root—he could begin to transform behavior and avoid the problem altogether. The ceiling didn't change—his perspective did!

Third, repeat the positive pattern several times at first. In this case, I made him go back downstairs and come up more slowly three times. It sounds silly, but the repetition helps create a memory in your body, mind, and spirit—one that will slowly become a natural part of your pattern. Finally, support your repatterning efforts with other methods like meditation, wherein you can visualize the transformation as an achieved fact. Together with diligence, I can nearly guarantee you'll achieve reasonable success.

Happiness

Happiness never decreases by being shared. —BUDDHA

Life, liberty, and the pursuit of happiness—those of us who live in the United States see these things as undeniable rights. Even so, it would seem that life's inevitable problems are constantly trying to wear away our pursuit of happiness, to the point where many of us feel plain beat—as if happiness is overrated. Sometimes Granny agrees. I think we create perceptions of what constitutes happiness without necessarily understanding what will make us *truly* happy!

Be that as it may, our ancestors (being quite a bit like us) also pursued happiness zealously on both a mundane and metaphysical level. Mundanely they worked very hard to make their lives fulfilling and provide a good home for their children. Magickally they devised all manner of charms and spells to encourage ongoing happiness. For example, a person might carry blue lace agate to generate joy, an amethyst to banish sorrow, aquamarine to soothe emotions, or a rose quartz for overall happiness (especially with self).

Of course, the ancients didn't stop there. They looked to the plant kingdom for happiness helpers too. Here is just a short list of some of the recommendations I found on this topic for you to try in your own workings:

- *Catnip:* Grow it near the home to promote joy, or carry a sprig with you.

- *Cumin:* Burn it as part of incense to bring happiness to a relationship.

- *Hawthorn flowers:* Carry in a charm for mirth.

- *Hyacinth:* Use in aromatherapy for delight.

- *Lavender:* Grown or used as an aromatic, this promotes a gentle cheerfulness and sense of peace.

- *Lily of the valley:* Put these in the room of someone who is feeling sad to lift their spirits.

- *Lemon:* Used in cooking, this fruit promotes happiness, especially between two people.

- *Marjoram:* Cook with this to banish the blues.

- *Peach:* Blossoms kept by your door keep sadness away, or you can eat peaches to internalize joy.

- *Quince:* Eat to encourage gaiety.

- *Raspberry:* Use a raspberry aromatic oil on your light bulbs to cheer your entire home.

- *Saffron:* Steep a little in water and use to asperge any area where negativity lingers. It lifts the vibrations.

- *Sugar cane:* Nibble a bit to make life sweeter.

Finally, one other thing I do around the house sometimes is to include some magick with my cleaning routines. Specifically, I sweep out any lingering melancholy, and then sprinkle some lavender outside my doorway to welcome peace and joy. Try this at least once a month to keep the vibrations in your house upbeat.

Healing

Healing is a matter of time, but it is sometimes also a matter of opportunity. —Hippocrates

Wholeness of body, mind, and spirit is something very important to witches (and most spiritual practitioners I know). It is believed by most Wiccans and neo-Pagans that if someone suffers spiritually it can manifest in their mind or body, that suffering of the body can and does affect mind and spirit, and so forth. Thus when we undertake any form of healing regimen, it isn't just handled on a physical level, but also a metaphysical one (using the "as within, so without" axiom as a guiding principle).

Perhaps this is why many neo-Pagans look to holistic options as part of their healing regimen. The term *holistic* means the sum of the parts add up to the whole, and perhaps something even greater than the whole. In short, since humans are a triune system, no one part can be truly healthy without the other parts being likewise so. Similarly, we will never truly be whole as citizens of this earth until our planet is whole (we are part of that cosmic system).

In any case, our quest for healing does not stop with holistics. We can also consider magickal methods to support the others we're undergoing. Note that I used the word *support*. I do not recommend anyone blithely trust in one spell, ritual, or amulet to take care of physical or mental illnesses. These two aspects of self exist in the temporal world and need temporal attention.

Healing Components

So what items from the natural world have people used to promote healing energies? In reviewing global beliefs it seems like nearly everything was tried once or twice (probably because life spans were much shorter; that lead to greater experimentation). Here are some of the components that remained as part of our tradition after the trial and error process.

- *Crystals:* Historically crystals were carried as amulets, placed on the body to absorb sickness, tossed in water to carry away disease, and even powdered into potions. Amber was one of the most popular in that it was thought to capture illness similarly to the way it captured insects! Modern approaches to crystals and healing grew out of these ideas, but most often they're kept with a person to promote ongoing health or laid on the body to interact with the aura. In the case of the latter the type of crystal and its placement depends on the problem. Amethyst, for example, is thought to heal respiratory infection or spiritual maladies.

- *Herbs:* I will be talking about herbs more in the next category of this book; however, herbalism as a healing method mingles beautifully with magick since for a long time its efficacy was thought to be thanks to plant Spirits! While herbalism has defined results in the real world, the energy signature of herbs shouldn't be overlooked in how we apply them. Incense, potpourri, and amuletic bundles are all good options to help with this (while potions are okay, some may interact badly with more conventional medication).

- *Meditation/visualization/dream work:* By creating an image of wholeness and holding it in our minds, we begin to adjust our body's auric energies to mirror that pattern.

- *Affirmations:* Similar to using meditation, affirmations use the power of sound and word to create the pattern of health in and around our lives.

As with the rest of your practice, you will want to find an approach that has a strong personal significance and one that also makes sense considering your condition. For example, you might like using affirmations but they don't do much good if you have laryngitis! In this case, you could recite the positive words mentally instead of verbally so you don't aggravate the problem.

Herbs

Small herbs have grace.　　　—WILLIAM SHAKESPEARE

Among the ultimate of gifts from nature's supermarket, herbs are of great value to any Witch (and any student of the magickal arts). There are so many ways of adapting and applying herbal arts to magic that Granny says they're a nearly indispensable element in the witch's kit. There's one point that requires clarification, however, when we talk about herbs in any context. Many people think of herbs as the spices on a pantry shelf, and by dictionary definition an herb is a seed producing annual. Nonetheless, both domestic and herbal arts have not been limited in any way to either description. Nearly every plant has been placed under the umbrella category of herb (including weeds), along with various plant parts like flower petals, barks, seeds, berries, roots, vines, leaves, fruits, and nuts. So we're certainly not just talking about culinary spices here.

Even with the broadened definition, however, being a Cunning Person by nature (meaning frugal and practical in my approach—okay, downright cheap!), I usually turn to whatever is handy in my garden or pantry for herbal workings. Even up to one hundred years ago, that was the way of things (they didn't have quickie marts and bulk herb stores). So before you go hunting for something exotic, look to what's readily on hand, for the herb that has all the right energies for the task and the right form for whatever you're creating. For example, allspice berries are fine for potions and sachets (or for saturating with energy then tossing to water or wind) but they don't burn very well as incense unless you powder them. Similarly, bay leaves are great for writing wishes upon, but can overwhelm other aromatics in a blend.

Hints for Beginners

If you're new to magickal herbalism, there are a few helpful hints that will make your attempts more successful:

- Get to know your ingredients intimately and how they react in various environments. For example, fresh roses will take on a very nasty scent if you boil them at high temperatures or include any green parts when steeping in oils.

- When you're first starting to make oils or incense stick to no more than two or three key ingredients.

- Always add ingredients slowly so that the scent is pleasing and the energy properly balanced.

- Use organics whenever possible (inorganic chemicals such as many pesticides can skew magickal results).

- Give back to the Earth with thankfulness (remember if that storehouse gets used up or overly abused, you can't return to it!).

- Fresher is better, but if you're using dry or powdered herbs the potency is often greater due to concentration. Adjust your blends accordingly.

- Look to any personal folklore or superstitions in the way you utilize your herbs. Since you know, for example, that red roses symbolize love, they make a good ingredient for a love sachet, potion, or incense (but would need to be dried for the latter application).

- Be careful about any herbs that could be harmful to your pets (refer to a list of poisons so you don't leave the wrong things lying out).

- If home grown, take into account the shift in energies that various growing conditions can have on your plants. For example, "fire"-oriented plants like marigolds will have some residual water energies during highly rainy years.

I honestly cannot think of one magickal process to which herbs cannot be added in a creative and meaningful way. Strew them around the sacred space to mark your circle, burn some in the brazier, place them on the altar, mix them into incense for meditations, steep them in potions, release them to the four winds with your wishes. Really, it's up to you!

Humor

The sense of humor is the oil of life's engine. Without it, the machinery creaks and groans. No lot is so hard, no aspect of things is so grim, but it relaxes before a hearty laugh. —GEORGE S. MERRIAM

Anyone who spends more than ten minutes with me knows that I use humor as both a coping mechanism and a teaching tool. Laughter is great soul food and it also brings people into harmony with each other. When you laugh, those little energy bricks that have built up from normal daily pressures and activities fall neatly to the ground (and stay there unless you choose to pick them up again). Thus, Granny highly recommends finding a way to bring more laughter into your life every day. No, this doesn't mean becoming the proverbial class clown or laughing at inappropriate moments—rather, it's a way of looking at life that allows you to see the humor and to use that positive energy.

Aura Tickling

There are two different approaches I use for lifting the energy in my aura and encouraging good humor. The first is to visualize a flood of very tiny pink, blue, and white bubbles filling the auric envelope. If you can think about how small soap bubbles feel as they slide against your skin, you have some idea as to how this will feel in your aura. It literally tickles.

As the bubbles move around, they gather up any negative energy. You'll see some of them change into brown or black. When this happens, release those bubbles from your visualization into the ground. Continue until the bubbles that come into the aura and those that leave are the same clean hue. Then go watch a good sitcom or read the comics!

The other method I use is that of taking some burning herbs and moving them into my living space and aura using a large feather. A feather symbolizes lightheartedness to me (and it's also something that tickles the skin). Depending on your perspective you can move the smoke around counterclockwise to banish those energies you don't want, or move clockwise to welcome the new energy. When things are really bad I use a cleansing incense counterclockwise, then an uplifting one clockwise. For cleansing try lemon, sage, cedar, or sweetgrass. For improving the mood try lavender, lily of the valley, and marjoram.

Image Magick (*Poppets*)

A rock pile ceases to be a rock pile the moment a single man contemplates it, bearing within him the image of a cathedral.

—Antoine de Saint-Exupéry

Image magick has existed for a very long time. It's based on the Laws of Sympathy and Similars (see *Sympathy and Similars*) in that the practitioner uses the image of someone or something to affect that person/item magickally. In particular poppets (dolls) have been used this way since about 1900 B.C.E. (Egypt). The materials for such creations varied greatly and included clay, wax, wood, dough, cloth, a sheaf of wheat, and even sometimes carved vegetables (like a potato).

Typically the poppet is formed very conscientiously so that it resembles the person or thing it's meant to affect. For example, women in China carried the image of a baby on their backs when they wished to conceive. Russian, French, and Swedish women have very similar customs. It's more than likely that the images on the Western wedding cake have their roots in these types of fertility rites.

In the case of the wheat, it's obvious that unless you do some serious shaping the wheat will not look like a person or thing. Rather, the last sheaf of wheat gathered from a field represents the spirit of the harvest—and it needs no other shape. This sheaf was often named things like old woman, wheat bride, or corn queen to indicate its importance, and usually it was kept very safe until the next planting season when it would be returned to the Earth by way of a land blessing.

Throughout Europe dolls and various images were once commonly used as charms. For instance, a sickly child might be given a poppet filled with healthful herbs to play with. Later on, that doll might be burned so that the child's sickness was likewise destroyed (note that this is a type of disease transference rite). Alternatively two dolls might be used as a love spell by tying them together using a red string, then keeping them in a safe place. And for image magick? It was everywhere, and indeed our custom of wearing little charms on bracelets comes from this old, honored method. Each one has specific meaning (like an anchor for foundations, a house for a happy home, and so forth).

As with any type of magick, the most important thing about the image you use is its meaningfulness to the overall goals you have in mind. Additionally, whatever happens to that image in your ritual or spell should be sensually significant to what you want to have happen in terms of manifestation. For example, if you've made a poppet of someone who is gossiping you might place a piece of tape over its mouth in your spellcraft to silence those lies (note: make sure you have the right person here!). If your pet is ill, you might take a picture of him or her and dab healing oils on it, or keep it in cotton on your altar to offer comfort. In this way both the object and the action mirror intention, which is what creates the energy you're seeking.

Jobs

The best thing workers can bring to their jobs is a lifelong thirst for learning. —JACK WELCH

It's a workaday world. But when you don't have a job or aren't happy in the one you've got, I suggest combining a healthy dose of magick to whatever mundane efforts you're making. Typically people come to me looking for three types of spells in this category: one to help them locate the right job, one to get a raise or promotion, and one to decrease tensions or negativities at the work place. Here are samples of each for you to try or adapt:

Finding Work

When I'm job hunting I like to use candle magick to support the effort. Take out a red candle for luck and a green candle (money). Place these somewhere near your front door. Light them and open the door saying:

> *I welcome success*
> *I welcome prosperity*

I welcome a new job
I welcome stability

Leave the door open and the candles burning while you hunt through the want ads, make calls, and mail resumes. The open door represents "welcome" and an open pathway for the energy. If you want, you can use the wax to seal your envelopes so each carries the magick you're creating.

Promotions / Raises

For this activity I'd like you to make a pseudo business card for yourself with your current title (if you want a raise) or the position for which you're vying (if you're trying for a promotion). Dab this with a money-oriented aromatic like mint, cinnamon, or orange. Charge it saying this incantation or something similar four times (the number of Earth, foundations, and prosperity):

My work is sound, my efforts firm
Through it a _____ (raise/promotion) I'll earn

Now take this card and put it in the highest safe place possible (like on top of a bookshelf, behind a mirror, above a door lintel, or something similar). The idea is that you want upward movement, and this action mirrors that goal. Leave it there until the magick manifests; then carry the card with you as an ongoing charm for success.

Improving Work Atmosphere

Aromatherapy is a great way to improve the work environment very subtly. Few people think anything of smelling cologne, perfume, a small bundle of potpourri, or a gathering of flowers. Here's a list of some of the scents that you can consider using alone or in combination:

- *Bergamot:* Decreases tension or weariness

- *Chamomile:* Alleviates resentment

- *Frankincense:* Offsets anxiety

- *Jasmine:* Supports confidence

- *Lavender:* Calms nerves

- *Lemon:* Overall cleanser

- *Orange:* Calming influence

- *Sage:* Purification

- *Sandalwood:* Decreases pressure, improves confidence

One really effective way to use aromatherapy is dabbing essential oils around your work area. This basically "marks" the space as yours, and also releases the vibrations you most need into the air nearby.

Justice (*Legal Matters*)

> *I shall not submit to injustice from anyone. I shall conquer untruth by truth.*
> —MAHATMA GANDHI

Life is not always fair or just. We face many situations where the scales of Lady Justice seem sorely out of balance. And in a society that's obsessed with a variety of legal matters, it's good to have a pocket full of magick as an ally.

Let's consider a situation where equity hasn't been served. In this case I recommend trying to spiritually return things to a balanced state as opposed to looking for outright revenge (which also puts energy off kilter). In your mind's eye see the situation as it stands on one half of a giant scale. Put in as many pertinent details as possible to create a three-dimensional image.

Next, slowly begin reconstructing the situation in the most perfect way possible on the other half of the scale. As you do, you'll notice the scale moving into balance but the negative side will be slightly heavier. Finally, reach out with one hand into the image and knock part of the negative side off (especially any key parts that caused the inequity). Now the scale is balanced. Hold that image of balance in your heart while you work on mundane levels.

By the way, if you'd like to create a charm to take with you into that situation (or into court) some of the components used historically include buckthorn, celandine, hickory, marigold, amethyst, and bloodstone. Put bits of wood in a pouch with the marigold and one or both of the stones and charge it saying:

> *Justice with me come, and dance*
> *Help me restore the balance*
> *Equity to me bear*
> *Let all proceedings be wholly fair.*

Carry the charm with you until things resolve themselves.

Kindness

Whoever said, "Practice random acts of kindness" must have been a wise Witch in the making! There is always room for a little extra kindness in the world. It makes so many things in our life easier and more enjoyable. This spell is designed to help you express your thoughtfulness to others, and to encourage an overall air of consideration in and around your life.

I think of kindness as a warm, welcoming energy and something that seems to naturally encourage more of the same (meaning it increases outward geometrically). Therefore, try baking this good-natured bread. The lemon encourages good feelings, the orange overall happiness, and the pineapple is for hospitality.

> 1 loaf self-rising frozen bread dough
> ¼ teaspoon lemon zest
> ¼ teaspoon powdered orange rind
> 1 tablespoon butter

1 tablespoon honey
½ tablespoon pineapple juice

Follow the directions on the bread dough for defrosting
and letting the bread rise the first time. Knead in the
lemon zest and orange rind, allowing the bread to rise
again. Bake in a well-oiled pan (again following the baking directions provided). During the last ten minutes of
baking, melt the butter, honey and pineapple juice together to make a glaze. Brush this on top of the bread at
five-minute intervals. Cool and serve with a smile!

By the way, if you don't have time to fuss with bread, try mixing orange
juice and pineapple juice together with a slice of lemon. It's a very re-
freshing "potion" that you can serve to family and guests alike to promote a considerate atmosphere.

Kinship *(Tribal Connection)*

*Call it a clan, call it a network, call it a tribe, call it a family. Whatever
you call it, whoever you are, you need one.*   —JANE HOWARD

Over the past five years it's become exceedingly apparent to Granny that
people have become disconnected. We live hundreds (if not thousands)
of miles apart from family and friends, and often find ourselves feeling
lost in the human sea. This is most strongly evidenced in our youth.
Unlike the time when we were still living among close-knit tribes, chil-

dren do not necessarily have a sense of belonging. They are not growing up knowing what career they will have (and in fact wonder if there will be gainful employment at all!). Combine that with the world's dwindling resources and it's little wonder that many of our youths and adults alike succumb to apathy. It's easier to feel nothing.

So how exactly do we go about fixing this problem? At least part of the answer comes from finding what Granny calls "family of the heart"—these are people with whom you have strong, intimate connections but no blood ties. While there is your home Tribe of family, and your peer school Tribe, and the work Tribe—this personal group is one in which spiritual seekers often find the connections the strongest. Why is that? Because you can't choose family or coworkers, but you *do* choose these people!

The ways in which to help yourself find the right people for that Tribe depends on what feels right to you. Pray, do a ritual, cast a spell, visualize. Stay awake and aware; listen and watch. As you do you'll begin to meet kindred spirits that you feel like you want to keep close. Listen to that instinct and begin taking steps to honor that emotion.

How exactly do you accomplish that honoring? The number-one way is by being thoughtful. Remember important occasions. Give little tokens or cards for no reason whatsoever. Touch, hold, and smile. Listen, share, and talk. Know when to give your Tribe space and when to hold them close.

The Importance of Tribe

You might call it a community, a clan, a household or a karmic circle, but, no matter the name, Tribe is important for:

- *Nurturing, comforting, and providing other emotional needs for one another*
- *Offering support physically, mentally, and spiritually*
- *Providing constructive criticism and an equal amount of due praise*
- *Keeping people united despite distance*

- *Creating strength in numbers*
- *Honing the self as part of a greater whole*
- *Sustaining the larger community of tribes and by extension the earth*
- *Ministering to each other (making sure no one falls through the cracks)*
- *Manifesting community goals and meeting needs*
- *Recording histories and stories for future generations (preserving tradition)*
- *Inspiring each other's visions*

Next, invite Spirit into your tribe as a participant. Remember your extended family in your prayers and on your altar. Also, and perhaps most important of all, *pay attention to the details*. Little things mean a lot, folks. Knowing that one person hates onions, another loves the color blue, and another still is allergic to lavender may all sound like no big deal but they truly matter. Each time you remember these little things people know you're paying attention and that you truly care enough to do so—to invest yourself in that relationship.

When something goes awry, fix it immediately. Don't wait until the problem becomes impossible to repair. Anytime we're part of a group, even of individuals who do not know each other, it's inevitable that problems and misunderstandings will arise. You may even have days when you love each other, but don't like each other very much. That's okay. You know what? The ancient tribes didn't always get along either! The key here is that you care enough to make the effort to heal and remain whole together.

In the end the concept of kinship, community, and Tribe really boils down to the Native American saying "and all my relations." This phrase is added to the end of prayers akin to the "good of all." On the surface that doesn't sound like a lot, but the implications are enormous. To work for the good of all—to bless, honor, respect, and be grateful for all our relations of blood and spirit—that is the reality of spiritual kinship, and it's a reality well worth working toward.

Kitchen Witchery

And, indeed, is there not something holy about a great kitchen? The scoured gleam of row upon row of metal vessels dangling from hooks or reposing on their shelves till needed with the air of so many chalices waiting for the celebration of the sacrament of food. And the range like an altar, yes, before which my mother bowed in perpetual homage, a fringe of sweat upon her upper lip and the fire glowing in her cheeks.

—Angela Carter

Granny is a Kitchen Witch from *waaaay* back. To me, there is nothing more satisfying and pleasant than puttering in the pantry and whipping up a little magick as I go. What's interesting, however, is that I've met some people who think kitchen magick is limited to the kitchen, and others who feel that this cunning art is too simple to work. *Bah* to both!

The basic principles of Kitchen Witchery apply to all aspects of life and certainly aren't wimpy in any shape or form. These principles include:

- Life is an act of worship.

- Treat all things like implements of the altar (i.e., everything in this world has magickal potential if you learn to perceive that potential and then enable it).

- Simplicity, creativity, and personalization = power and manifestation.

- Laughter and playfulness are sacraments.

- Spirituality must be blended with everyday life or it lacks true meaning and power.

- Remain connected to your principles and ethics—kitchen magick always honors these in word and deed.

- How you do things is not nearly as important as *why*.

- Reciprocity in all things is a keynote to success.

- Honor, respect, and gratitude are the trinity on which a sound spiritual life is built.

- Your body and your home are sacred spaces: treat them accordingly.

In reading this list I think you can see why I believe that Kitchen Witchery has a place not only throughout one's home, but also one's daily life. Kitchen magick developed with everyday people trying to make their lives a little better. It's practical, frugal, wise, and ever-evolving with the times. This makes kitchen magick very vital and adaptable, which considering our fast-paced times and technological advances is very important. Better still, one need not be a kitchen witch to practice kitchen magicks!

Okay, so what is kitchen magick exactly? Ask ten witches and you're likely to get ten slightly different answers. Granny will share her own. To me kitchen magick is a hearth- and home-based system Our components are everyday items, found in and around that sacred space. Our processes reflect our everyday lives, and our magick meets everyday needs. Perhaps that sounds rather uninteresting and ordinary, but it truly is an extraordinary way of going through a day!

And what about the results obtained? They are as potent as any other form of magick so long as you trust in the process and understand the symbolism. Our society often reflects the idea that fancy = better, but that's simply not the case with a vision based, will-driven system like the Craft. While there are times when (as they say), "it's all in the details," there are an equal number of times when releasing ourselves from complexity allows us to turn our minds wholly on the magick we're producing. I jokingly call this flying by the seat of my broomstick, but find it both liberating and time smart. If your schedule is anything like mine, you also may find such methods appealing.

Some recommended reading on this topic include my *Kitchen Witch's Cookbook, Victorian Grimoire, Bubble-Bubble-Toil & Trouble,* and *Charmed Life.* Also *Everyday Magick* by Dorothy Morrison is a great primer.

Knot Magick

We learn the rope of life by untying its knots.   —JEAN TOOMER

Historically speaking knots were used for a wide variety of mundane and magickal functions. Historians like Herodotus (400 B.C.E.) used them as a way of memorizing specific chronicles. People also used them to mark time for travel, to count the days between important festivals, and to follow lunar observances for various rituals. The Hebrews even went so far as to make knots into an alphabet and writing system.

For our purposes knot magick's power lies in its strong symbolic value. We see again and again in older spell books how a knot was used to bind disease and spirits, to loose passions or to conjure up a specific type of weather. To the basic process of tying or releasing, numerology, color associations, and incantations were typically added to symbolize and specify where the energy was being directed.

Now, since modern folks have ample access to string, yarn, laces, ribbons, scarves, and other items that can easily be tied, knot magick becomes a wonderfully accessible method. Here's a brief list of historical applications for knot magick:

- *Knot amulets:* It's no coincidence that the word *magician* in Russian means "knot tier," just as it does in Hebrew. Similarly, in Aramaic texts the word *qami'a* (meaning knot) became the word for amulet. In Indonesia people still call the process of making charms "knot tying."

  Since amulets are considered protective, a knot or series of knots (the number being symbolic) would be created to fight off sickness, protect well-being, keep soldiers from getting wounded, or promote children's safety. To be most effective these knots had to be worn (preferably near the area where they'd do the most good) or carried.

- *Curative knots:* Babylonians and Rumanians alike used knots as a curative. Typically, cords with the appropriate number of knots (this depended on the sickness) would be created and laid upon the problematic area for a set number of days (to gather and hold the sickness within). Afterward the knot was typically ritually destroyed, tied to a tree (disease transference), or tossed in running water moving away from the patient to overcome or move away the illness.

- *Birthing knots:* Australian midwives would loosen a knotted willow branch to help release the milk flow of a newly nursing mother. In many other areas of the world it's customary for the midwife and her attendants to open doors, windows, buttons, and anything knotted to open the birth canal.

- *Protective knots:* We find these in many places, but in Assyria one is specifically instructed to use white wool tied to the bed and black wool neatly wound around the left hand to be well guarded against spells.

- *Memory knots:* Tying a knot in a scarf, handkerchief, or even around your finger is an ancient charm so that you will not forget something important. When you need to remember—open the knot to release the memory.

- *Love knots:* Among the most prevalent use of knots, which is still obvious by the use of the phrase "tying the knot" in relationship to marriage. As early as Roman times men and women alike were tying knots to ensure love. In Sweden people went so far as to have very specifically shaped knots for engagement, friendship, and passion.

- *Promissory knots:* The word *notary* comes from *notador*, meaning tier of, or observer of, knots! This came about due to a custom in the Middle Ages of witnessing a contract by using knots that would be bound when the contractual issue was completely agreed upon.

- *Religious knots:* It's not uncommon even today to find various religious orders using knots to subtly reveal initiation or rank within that order. The knot gently reminds the wearer of his or her vows, and also speaks to those who understand his or her proper place in the scheme of things.

- *Weather knot:* Even well into Shakespeare's day, sailors trusted in wind and weather knots to help them on long sea voyages. If a small wind was needed, one knot would be released. A full wind required two knots. Only the foolish, however, would open all three, as that would bring a full gale due to being greedy.

As you can see, there are many ways to use these ideas just as they stand, or adapt them a bit to more personal goals. Don't forget to use color symbolism when choosing what you're going to tie or loosen, as well as numeric correspondences.

Additionally, if you wish you can tie objects into a knot. Choose the object for its symbolic value. When you open the knot, the object is released to visually support the magickal flow of energy. For example, a feather or other lightweight object is ideal for wind magick because it moves with the winds and can symbolize your magick taking wing!

Learning and Knowledge *(Memory)*

Don't limit a child to your own learning, for he was born in another time. —RABBINIC SAYING

Learning and being able to apply what we learn is a great human capacity. Granny would go one step further to say that exhibiting what we learn in word and deed (hopefully with wisdom) is the sign of a person whose Path is moving forward. But what about those times when you feel like you just can't wrap your head around a concept, you're having trouble concentrating, or find that the information you *should* know seems elusive to your memory? We all have these moments, and this is yet another time when your magickal practices can help you.

To devise spells and charms for this purpose, first let's look to some of the key components traditionally used. We have walnuts (that look a bit like a brain), rosemary to improve memory retention, coffee or tea for alertness, anything colored yellow or gold to support the conscious, rational mind, fluorite for the positive application of what we learn, and of course any items that we associate with learning like a notepad or computer. Combining these isn't difficult.

Fluorite Learning Charm

I'm particularly fond of fluorite because it's very reasonably priced, highly available, and has a very reassuring color. To make this charm you'll need one piece of fluorite (perhaps one shaped like a pyramid) and a bit of rosemary oil. Rub a little of the oil on your stone during the noon hour (a time that accentuates rationality) saying:

> *Knowledge is for what I yearn*
> *In my heart, a fire burns*
> *Help me in my quest to learn*

Repeat the incantation eight times for personal transformation, and then carry the charm with you whenever you're in a difficult learning situation. Rub the stone a bit and mentally repeat the incantation again to release a little of the magick. When you've used it seven times, recharge it.

Training Tincture

Make a cup of coffee or tea (your preference) in a yellow cup. Enjoy this at the outset of your day, blessing it by saying something like:

> *What I hear commit to me*
> *By my will this spell is free*
> *The information to my mind*
> *In this cup the magick bind*
> *And when taken sip by sip*
> *Bring the knowledge to my lips*

Sip slowly, letting the magick saturate your being before you go to your studies.

Love

Tell me who you love, and I'll tell you who you are.

—Creole proverb

Love is one of those emotions with which we have "love-hate" relationships. When we're in love, the world seems rosy. When we're out of love, we gripe but still yearn for it. If that weren't confusing enough, there are all kinds of love—the love of a pet, a child, a job, an art form. All these dimensions makes love a very confusing creature no matter how adept or wise we may be. So in considering our love magick, we need to take love out of the box, and really examine what it is we're seeking. Do we want romance? Warmth? Friendly love? Gentle, lasting love?

Love Walks with Me

Once you know the type of love desired, it become much easier to welcome that energy in your life. My favorite love spell is an incredibly easy one, and it's useful to any sort of love—just change the color or type of flower petals to reflect your desire. For example, red rose petals would be for passionate love, while pink ones mixed with lavender flowers might be used for a gentle, friendly love. Take a handful of your chosen flower petals outside your doorway and sprinkle them on the path leading to your home. Open the door to welcome love. Reserve one or two petals to put in your shoe so love walks with you!

Self-Love

Self-love seems to be one of those things we have trouble developing. In part we worry about our egos getting overly puffed up. And while that's a valid concern, it's not a reason to overlook your needs as being secondary or unimportant. That's why one component in this charm is a mirror. See yourself honestly, but *see* the good too!

The other component is a pink quartz (rose) for gentle love. Now, put the mirror on a flat surface. Also get some glue. Look at your reflection; place the rose quartz in the center of that reflection and say:

> *I give myself love*
> *I accept love from me*
> *I am ready to give and receive love*

When the glue dries, wrap this in pink cloth so the stone isn't easily knocked off, and carry it with you.

Speaking of keeping love with you, Granny would like to share two more insights. We speak a lot in magickal circles about perfect love and perfect trust. Nonetheless, neither is ever truly perfect—because humans are not perfect. Please be careful and be sure the people toward whom you give such great gifts deserve them. Also, don't forget to love yourself. I know it sounds hokey, but someone who truly loves Self is far more capable of giving and receiving love, with a heart of gratitude. You are the most important person in the world in your karmic circle. Don't forget to give that person as much consideration as you would anyone else. You'll find your spiritual path benefits greatly from it.

> *There is great comfort and inspiration in the feeling of close human relationships and its bearing on our mutual fortunes—a powerful force, to overcome the "tough breaks" which are certain to come to most of us from time to time.*   —WALT DISNEY

Luck

Diligence is the mother of good luck. —BENJAMIN FRANKLIN

The wise Witch realizes that luck is dependent at least 70 percent on hard work. Even so, traditional magic suggests tons of ways that we can activate that last 30 percent for our benefit. When you really need a change, or would just like some improved good fortune, there are dozens of spells and charms to get the energies rolling in the right direction. The question then becomes how do you choose among them?

Well, interestingly enough the luck magick that our ancestors prescribed usually had some type of focus (luck with money, luck with relationships, etc.). So, the first step to choosing luck components would be exploring a little more of their historical applications, and determining whether those applications make sense to you. A second approach would be to consider the luck lore handed down to you from your family. If your mother or grandfather carried a rabbit's foot, lucky coin, or religiously avoided walking under ladders, you may find yourself following that same belief out of habit. Nonetheless, since you already have a strong connection to the belief, there's no reason not to apply it to your magick too.

A third approach that I often suggest to my students is to change their daily routine a bit. Try to move through the house clockwise, follow a route to work that bears to the right, and so forth. The sunwise pattern is thought to encourage not only luck but also blessings (thus our use of clockwise dancing and movement to generate positive energy). Additionally, since bad luck tends to come in cycles or streaks, by changing your pattern you can break the back of that negative energy—easily and effectively!

Here's a brief list of luck-enhancing components for your reference:

- Black-eyed peas (best if consumed on any New Year's celebration).

- Put your right foot forward (this custom originated in Rome).

- Eat spiced rice for improved luck with your health (Japan).

- Turn a mirror outward, facing the direction in which you feel your bad luck originates (this is an adaptation of Feng Shui methods).

- Turn a piece of clothing inside out and wear it for the day (this, along with sitting backwards on a chair, is an old gambler's trick to turn luck's tide in their favor).

- Carry carnelian on Thursdays to improve your luck in communications, a turquoise on Saturdays for luck in travel.

- Wearing any solar symbol is said to improve overall blessings and luck (especially in times of danger).

- Never brag about your luck—it spoils the energy.

- Myrtle in your garden brings good fortune to all within the home and domestic joy.

- Carry jade to encourage luck in relationships (China).

- Victorians plucked an ash leaf and carried it for luck (only for that day). Ash wood is a good base for luck incense.

- Found keys should be kept and carried for luck in legal matters.

There are obviously hundreds (if not thousands) of other superstitions about luck. Take your time and find the ones you really like and to which you relate. It's a charming exploration of human thought and history, and one likely to yield some wonderful magick too!

Magick and Witchery

The universe is full of magical things, patiently waiting for our wits to grow sharper. —EDEN PHILLPOTTS

The village wise person often consulted people in matters of both mundane and spiritual import. Among the spiritual questions that comes up is: Is magick and witchcraft for *me* (often followed shortly thereafter with, Can I really do this?)? Let's look briefly at both questions.

Since you're reading this book, you've likely already answered the first question with a yes (and possibly also the second). But what about other people who will come to you with similar questions? What do you tell them? How do you help them make such an important choice without thumping your Book of Shadows?

This isn't an easy question because it's natural for people to be enthusiastic about something that's working on an intimate personal level. You might be tempted to just say, "Hey, dive in...the water's fine" but that's not the best approach. I typically tell people to read everything they can find for one full year. If possible, go to a gathering or conference. Meet people from as many Paths as you can, and ask questions. If at some point during this year something deep within resonates with what you're hearing and seeing, then I'd say take the next step. On the other hand, if they find nothing that makes sense and inspires, then wait. Magick has been around for thousands of years. If it's truly right for someone, it will be there tomorrow.

As for whether someone can work magick, my answer is *of course!* It won't be anything like Hollywood imagery, but in my opinion magick is the birthright of every human being. Some will be better at it than others, which is true of any art, but everyone can experience a degree of success. Generally the amount of that success is directly proportional to the time and energy you put into it on all levels of being!

What happens from this point forward is up to each person, but Granny would like to offer some advice. Take it slow and steady. Listen to the rhythm that exists in your heart and follow at that pace. Spirituality and magick isn't about keeping up with anyone else, it's about knowing yourself and honoring the divine within.

Spirituality Components

If you're looking for some components that have been used historically to help improve spiritual focus, this list is a good starting point:

- Cinnamon
- Sandalwood
- Gardenia
- Lepidolite
- Corn
- Coconut
- Honey
- Salt
- Frankincense (often blended with myrrh)
- Lotus
- Sugulite
- Amethyst
- Olives
- Date
- Saffron
- Squash

And as you move along your Path, don't forget from where you've come. I often see people musing over quote-unquote newbie Witches (novices) some of whom have pretty odd ideas about what constitutes Wicca and magick. But each of us at one time was "young"—we didn't understand the basics, and *all* of us are still learning. Maintaining that perspective makes for gentler, kinder, and wiser interactions. The truth is that we need each other and we can learn from each other, even novices who remind us of the power of hope and enthusiasm.

Finally, if the day comes that you feel called to move in a different direction, don't mourn that moment. Magick is meant to bend and change, and sometimes that even means our Path. Celebrate what has come before and what is yet to be. As the saying goes: It's all *good!*

Manifestation *(Movement)*

It takes a lot of courage to release the familiar and seemingly secure, to embrace the new. But there is no real security in what is no longer meaningful. There is more security in the adventurous and exciting, for in movement there is life, and in change there is power.

—ALAN COHEN

We talk a lot about magick "manifesting," but what exactly does that mean? What qualifies as manifestation? By dictionary definition, *manifest* means to make plain, to disclose to the public, to reveal. It also means to discover! In a spiritual sense this means the energy moves out of the astral, takes viable form in reality, and then we discover that reality.

The question is how do we go about encouraging manifestation? To answer this question Granny looks to the ancients, who often used ritualistic dance to nudge that process along. Ritual dancing consummates the connection between the spiritual and temporal. It provides an energy-generating medium, and it then offers a way for the practitioner to express magickal fulfillment as realized (in symbolic form). In fact, so important was ritual dancing that some myths even say that without dance the movement (note the word here) of the Universe itself would cease.

For years I watched people at gatherings come to the fire and begin to move gently to the music, and eventually lose themselves to that spiraling motion. They embraced the rhythm and flames as much as each other, and it was beautiful. I don't know what held me back from that for so long, but now that I've finally returned to celebrating dance as part of my spirituality, I can tell you honestly that it's a help with both manifestation and moving energy equally well. They are, in fact, part of each other. Without movement, manifestation cannot happen!

Whether or not you consider yourself someone with "rhythm"... whether or not you're coordinated and graceful...whether or not you've ever had a dance class, I am here to confirm the truth in this African saying: If you can walk; *you can dance.* Dancing is part of your spirit. If you trust in ancient philosophy, specifically Pythagorean, then you can feel comforted in knowing that even the cosmos dances and sings as each sphere moves through the sky. If something so huge can manage a dance to celebrate life's ongoing movement and manifestations, so can we!

So how exactly can you use dance to help with manifestation? First, consider the theme of the magick involved and then design a pattern for your dance that reflects the magick from beginning to completion. In some ways, this is like an elaborate pantomime, but one that develops slowly through the dances movements, building energy. Combine that movement with visualization, incense, music—and you have a multi-sensual experience, and a very personalized one.

Dancing the Dance

1. Warm up is very important on all levels of your being (physical, emotional, and spiritual). Do those all-important motivational checks, and make sure that you're not stressed, ill, or out of sorts before you begin.

2. Move into your dance area gently, treating it as sacred space. If you wish, call the quarters before you begin.

3. Take the time to become fully aware of your body and focus your mind on the spiritual energy you're wishing to support.

4. Release yourself to the symbolism and movements, letting all your senses guide you.

5. Trust the leadings of Spirit and translate them into your movements.

6. Let the dance naturally rise to a crescendo.

7. Release the energy toward its goal, then slow and ground trusting in your magick.

At the culmination of the dance, your movements state victory and completion—you are effectively mirroring the manifestation desired by changing auric and physical energy patterns. By the way, if you find yourself wanting for symbolic movements, simply move clockwise in your dance for positive energy, and counterclockwise to turn away (or decrease) negative energy.

Manners (*Courtesy*)

Our inheritance of well-founded, slowly conceived codes of honor,
morals, and manners, the passionate convictions which so many hundreds
of millions share together of the principles of freedom and justice, are
far more precious to us than anything which scientific discoveries could
bestow.   —WINSTON CHURCHILL

I gotta admit it...Granny puts high value on manners. As I travel, I meet so many young people who have no idea how to say "please" or "thank you," let alone "sir" or "ma'am." This trend is highly disturbing because it means that we as a society are losing sight of each other in this urban sea of humanity, and in turn we're losing the little courtesies that improve the way we're received. So how do we start regaining ground here?

The first step is going back to the adaptation and alertness activities earlier in this book. If we're becoming numb to other people's space and needs, alertness can help that. Once we're more aware, the next step is being flexible enough to change our habits from apathetic ones to active, positive ones. Additionally, if we pay particular attention to our communications we can weave affirmations into our courtesies!

Courtesy Charm

If you're looking for something portable to encourage mindful communications and politeness, I suggest a little container filled with salt. In Arabia, taking an oath by salt meant that a guest would be thoughtful and never overextend his stay. It also meant he would abide by prevalent house manners and traditions. That combined with the phrase "salt of the earth" provides good foundational symbolism for this component.

Bless the salt by saying something like:

> *Let none of my words harm or bite*
> *Let me extend courtesy with all my might*
> *From this moment on, all interactions be polite!*

Take a pinch of the salt out and scatter it to the winds whenever you find yourself slipping. Repeat the incantation mentally or out loud to improve the immediate effect.

Masks and Costumes

In the world through which I travel, I am endlessly creating myself.
—Frantz Fanon

From the time when neolithic Shamans wore bone-and-hide masks to invoke or honor Spirits up to the antics of Jim Carrey's character in the film *The Mask*, the power of these kinds of tools has remained a part of human interactions, including spiritual ones. Typically, masks have been seen as a symbol of and focus for power, magic, and mystery. When anyone wears a mask, that person transforms. We can melt into another presence, another time, and know it as our own. Costumes work similarly.

Traditionally costumes and masks were made out of a variety of natural items including bark, beans, fur, ropes, shells, woven fabric, and feathers. Add to that list a variety of manmade items that could be considered by a clever Witch, such as: paper, glitter, ribbons, noodles, candy, and buttons. This gives you a great variety from which to fashion the representation you need for your ritual.

Why go to all the trouble? The power of a costume or a mask lies not in the item, but in how it intersects with our conscious and sub-conscious mind. Whether we're wearing a mask or viewing it, a connection is made between what we see and what it represents. In other words your artistic display helps both the participants and the wearer of the mask make the transition away from the mundane into the spiritual. It helps us believe in what we see. In the magickal context this means that your friend and priestess "Mary" is no longer that person, but is now transformed into the Goddess or other Power.

Here are some other ways you can use masks and costumes to improve the overall visual impact of your magick:

- Design them to honor and uplift specific spirits with which you're working (such as animal guides).

- Make four masks to represent the elements/quarters of the sacred space, or perhaps one for each season with a matching robe.

- Create accoutrements that represent the goal of your spell in realized form. Donning them becomes an acceptance of that energy.

- Fashion complete outfits that represent your patron God or Goddess (this is an excellent way to honor and commune with him or her for Drawing Down the Sun or Moon rituals).

Remember that your costumes need not be fancy to be wholly functional (Clark Kent taught us that!). What's important is that the end result puts you (and anyone else participating) in the right frame of mind for the work ahead.

Meditation

Let us all to meditation   —WILLIAM SHAKESPEARE

The word *meditate* has interesting linguistic roots. Originally it meant *to measure*, which gives the phrase "measuring something up" whole new meaning. When we meditate we retrain our minds to focus on one specific thing (unless you're working with various Eastern methods where the goal is emptiness, the void). In this mental forum you can turn over a concept, problem, or situation and look at it from a distance. More important, you can internalize and/or transform those perspectives. This is, therefore, a very valuable tool in the Witch's kit, but one with which many people struggle.

Why the difficulty? Because our minds are used to multitasking and handling numerous thoughts and actions simultaneously. Nonetheless, don't be deterred by that. You will find that you already know something about meditation, even if you think you don't. Have you ever gotten so engrossed in a project that someone entered the room without your notice? This focus is a kind of meditation. Also, there are no particular "correct" positionings for meditation (no need to look like a pretzel). In fact, in some traditions walking, swimming, dancing, and other forms of movement are used as meditative vehicles to put the energy into motion!

Meditative Helps and Hints

1. *Breath:* Breathing patterns are central to nearly all meditative methods. I tell my students to breathe slowly and evenly, so that the end of one breath becomes the beginning of the next in an unbroken cycle. The inbound breath is one of acceptance, while the outbound one releases. Accept positive spiritual energy; release tension, worries, and unhealthy expectations.

2. *Positioning:* As I said before, you need not sit in a lotus position to meditate, but your position should make sense and be one that you can maintain without discomfort. If you're uncomfortable, that will distract your efforts. Stand or walk if your meditation has active elements; sit or lie flat for passive work (such as for rest and renewal).

3. *Sensual cues:* Sensual input is like the scenery in a play. It supports what's happening. Add some quiet music or incense. Wear comfortable clothing. Light candles to create a more spiritual ambiance.

4. *Visualizations:* Paint imagery in your mind's eye of the situation or focal point of the meditation. This imagery is something you can alter in positive ways. Think of it like watching a movie that you personally direct.

Bear in mind that meditation is a practice (and it takes *practice* to get good at it). Adding meditation to your day acts akin to a vitamin for your spirit. When you're sitting in the lavatory, taking a shower, walking the dog, or whatever—breathe and meditate (did I mention you don't have to close your eyes?). The time and effort are well worth it. I can promise that with due diligence those things on which you meditate, internalize and resolve will also manifest in your daily reality in powerful and personally meaningful ways.

Money *(Budget)*

Money will not make you happy, and happy will not make you money.
—GROUCHO MARX

While money might not buy happiness, this witch isn't naive. She knows that it sure makes things a lot easier! And while few people will ever get "rich" through magickal means, magick can (and does) help keep the financial flow on an even keel.

Good Karma Piggy Bank

The best type of money magick, seems to be the balance of giving to receiving. That's why I recommend what I call a Karmic Piggy Bank. To make a mockup of one, take a large bowl in which you secure a green candle with a dollar sign carved into it. In the bottom of the bowl place one seed coin (mark or wrap this coin in some manner so it doesn't get mixed up later). Now, every morning before you head out light the candle and focus on the exact amount of your financial need. Speak that amount into the candle four times, blowing it out on the fourth.

Next, when you come home that night, put any random change you have in the bowl. Repeat this daily, replacing the candle as necessary, until the bowl is full. This is the point at which the "giving" comes into play. Wrap up the change and give it to a charitable cause (be it a friend in need or a group whose land fund you want to support). Do not, however, remove the seed coin. This attracts the prosperity back to you threefold.

By the way, this little bit of giving to receive works with other needs in your life too. Just change the color and aroma of the candle to match your goal. For example, use red and roses for love, yellow and ginger for communication, white and mint for blessings, or orange and cinnamon for energy.

Fortune's Envelope

A slightly different approach of giving to receive, this spell begins with a bill of any denomination and a piece of paper whose color represents your goal. Write on it a word or phrase that states your need clearly. Fold this three times around the bill, speaking the words or phrase out loud, and put it in an envelope. Dab some money oil on the outside of the envelope (like mint).

Take the envelope to the post office and mail it to yourself. When it arrives in the mail, remove the paper and give that money to a good cause. Finally, burn the paper with your wishes, and expect the unexpected!

Networking

Man does not weave this web of life. He is merely a strand of it.
Whatever he does to the web, he does to himself. —Chief Seattle

Neo-Pagans pride themselves on their ability to network. The fact that our path was not "fashionable" for a long time forced us to create a dependable web of people that we could contact quickly with questions or needs. The Internet, of course, strengthened that ability. I have watched in awe as a request for assistance traveled around the world and got replies within hours (sometimes minutes). This is a great strength for us, and something that we should endeavor to maintain with due diligence.

In modern times the loss of ties, of Tribe, has been devastating on many levels. People feel lost, uncertain of their roles, and lack support. Our networking ability represents one way to keep that from happening in our community. By connecting, reconnecting, and staying connected, we build a strong infrastructure. Mind you, this process should be somewhat cautious. If you get a malicious, egotistical, selfish, or drama queen-type "spider" in the web, it can really muck things up. Choose your web strands wisely.

Protective Networking Amulet

Above and beyond the typical mundane necessities involved in maintaining our networks (like regularly reconfirming contact information), we can use magick to help support them as well. To create this amulet, you'll need to find a small dream catcher, preferably one that's undecorated. Additionally you'll need some protective beads (like eye agate), and one personal item. Adhere the personal token in the center of the web (this is your personal network). Attach the protective beads equally around the outside (twelve is good at the station points of the directions). Bless this token with an incantation like:

> *From strand to strand, watch over and protect*
> *All those with whom my heart connects*
> *Weave the network strong and sure*
> *Fill it with intentions, pure*
> *Each to each, All and one*
> *By my will, this spell's begun!*

Hang this near your computer or telephone (wherever you do the greatest amount of networking).

Offerings

The important thing is this: To be able at any moment to sacrifice what we are for what we could become. —CHARLES DU BOIS

While it might not be the most popular topic in this book, Granny thinks it's important to talk about the power of giving to receive (or giving just because it's the right thing to do!). The Earth and Spirit both bless us with numerous gifts. Offerings are a way of saying thank you. They're also a way to help manifest wishes and goals by releasing something you value.

Offerings take many forms. In Native American tradition there is the giveaway, where the gift goes to someone in need (or who has admired the item). I'm very fond of this approach as the offering blesses several people and still honors the Divine because you've listened to Spirit. Other offerings include those that are burnt, buried, tossed into water, divided among the clergy, and given to the land.

If you're working in the construct of the giveaway, you need not be limited to natural items. I would, however, strongly urge care in what types of offerings you leave outside the giveaway context. Stay with things nonharmful to the environment. We can look to our ancestors examples for ideas here including milk, wine, water, meat, woven fabric, and metals. Oh, and before I forget, music, song, and dance were considered good gifts for the Divine too—as Spirit rejoices in our abilities.

What other things should be considered in choosing offerings? In part the token should be meaningful, and if possible somehow represent why you're making the offering in the first place. The item also needs to make sense depending on the medium you're using for the offering. For example, don't try to burn treated fabrics. The result is usually smelly (not something that would please the Divine, let alone your neighbors).

When should you consider making an offering? Typically I do so in times of great need, or when magick manifests in a particularly wonderful way. In the case of the former, when we need money (for example) I offer some items that I love for sale at an auction house or on my event table. This begins generating an answer to my need, keeps me proactively involved as a cocreator, and still acts as a viable offering. And for the times when I'm thankful for my blessings? I share of them with others. Happiness is always better when spread around.

Opportunity

In the middle of difficulty lies opportunity.   —Albert Einstein

There's a great old adage that I adore: Don't be on the other side of town when your ship finally comes in! The key to opportunity magic is learning to recognize that "knock" and then answering it. Even more so, it's stepping through the doorway presented to you. Opportunity magick works on these things, along with helping to bring more opportunities your way (so you can practice).

Speaking of keys and doors, these two objects make wonderful symbols for opportunity magick.

Doorway Spell

The next time you wish to encourage opportunity, wait until the moon begins to wax (you want to increase openings). Then each night until the full moon go to your front door. Stand outside and knock three times saying:

> *With knock of one this spell's begun*
> *With knock of two, my will is true*
> *With the knock of three, opportunity to me*

Open the door, then say:

> *I welcome the Spirit of opportunity*
> *I open the way*
> *Hail and welcome.*

If you wish light a candle to honor the spirit of opportunity, and remember to be watchful at the end of this sequence. Very often something happens shortly thereafter that's your signal to move!

Unlock It!

This second spell needs only a key as a component (preferably one you don't need to use anymore). Dab this with an aromatic oil whose scent represents the area of your life in which you need an opportunity to manifest. As you rub it into the metal add an incantation like:

Around and within—the magick begins
Open the way—I charge you today
Show me the signs—opportunities be mine!

Take that key with you into the situation or circumstance that's the focus of the spell. Turn it in your pocket just before entering, and mentally recite the incantation again. Now, watch the energy turn in your favor!

Passion *(Lust)*

Before desiring something passionately one should inquire into the happiness of the man who possesses it.

—FRANÇOIS DE LA ROCHEFOUCAULD

Passion is another version of love on a very intense level. And as with any fire, if it burns too brightly it can be harmful, or go out altogether. So, while we need our passions, we also need to be able to measure them and mete them out so as not to get burned or have that passion die.

Let me back up for one moment. I should mention that when I say the word *passion,* most people think of sex. Nonetheless there are many things in life toward which we show passion and even lust. Some have passion for an art, some lust after money, others are passionate about their work, and others still lust after proverbial greener pastures. As you can see not all passion is negative, but lust tends to have a slightly gray side. So the charms, spells, and rituals for these two energies need to be carefully tempered.

Increasing Passion (any type)

Passion burns from deep within us. Therefore I like to use food magick to bolster it. In this case, marinate a skinless chicken breast in

191

strawberry juice and a hint of ginger. Strawberries promote passion, ginger provides energy, and the chicken keeps everything in a healthy balance. Cook or grill the chicken with a honey glaze (for life's sweetness). Each time you turn the chicken and baste with honey add an incantation like:

> *Fire, fire, burning bright*
> *The flame within is sheer delight*
> *Sweet and warm, a hint of compassion*
> *Fill this meal with the fires of passion*

Eat to internalize the energy (don't forget to focus your mind on the area of your life to which you want the energy applied).

Cooling Lust

Feeling just a little too enthusiastic toward someone (to the point of making him or her uncomfortable)? Has your passion toward a project gone way over the edge into dangerous territory? Try this little spell to help cool things down.

Take a piece of paper and write the specific area of your life in which lust is causing trouble. Rub the surface of your words with some body oil (this marks the paper with your personal energy signature). Place the paper on a plate or in a bowl and cover it with ice cubes saying:

> *Having acted the fool*
> *My passions now cool*
> *Whatever I felt,*
> *Decrease as this ice melts*

When the ice is completely melted toss both the water and the paper away (to likewise put the unwanted energy away from yourself).

Balancing Desire

In those moments when you don't want to completely turn off your passions, but rather bring them into equilibrium with the realities with which you're coping, create this charm. You'll need a square piece of paper or cloth on which you've drawn in equilateral cross (this represents the four corners, and symmetry). Place an onyx stone into the center of the paper saying:

> *North and South, East and West*
> *Powers hear my sincere behest*
> *Earth and air, fire and sea*
> *Bring to me your symmetry*

Bundle this up like a sachet and carry it with you.

Pathworking

> *Do not follow where the path may lead. Go instead where there is no path*
> *and leave a trail.* —RALPH WALDO EMERSON

Pathworking is a type of intense meditation that often takes place in a trancelike state. Before explaining this further, it's important to explain what a trancelike state is and what it is not. The Latin root word for trance means "to pass"—something that you go over or through. With this definition in mind, a trance state moves the individual through and beyond normal perceptions in order to experience a different type of awareness, one that is not limited by the physical world. In this dream-like condition, the practitioner can encounter animal guides and totems, and even become a channel for Divine energies.

All trances begin in meditation, and pathworking is one of the many applications for the meditative-trance state. While a person can meditate/visualize alone, Granny recommends that pathworking include a partner, for two reasons, the first of which is directly related to being in a trance. Individuals experienced with the trance state know that there are cues to traversing this inner space safely—entry points, exits, and landmarks. Even so, because this inner space is every bit as real as the world around, a person can lose his or her way. The job of a trance "spotter" is simply to guide you home and monitor your experience for signs of trouble.

The second reason for a pathworking partner is to have someone directing the activity (or minimally assisting at critical junctures). Why? Quite simply because rather than being defined from the outset, the "path" of the meditation unfolds one step at a time. It is difficult to do a lot of spontaneous thinking when your mind and spirit are heavily steeped in the energies of a meditation. This means that even if you've practiced the basic pattern of the path several times, you could forget the next step, get confused by the shifting nature of the path, or blank out altogether. At this juncture your pathworking partner steps in with simple verbal cues to keep the progression going.

As with meditation, there are some basic guidelines to help make your experience more successful and beneficial:

1. Have a specific goal in mind when designing and enacting the pathworking.

2. Choose symbols suited to that goal.

3. Design a defined entry, exit, and directional beacons for the path (ones that you can use with relative consistency. These act as astral landmarks).

4. Determine in what environment the visualization will take place mentally (and if that envisioned environment will transform as part of the pathworking). Note: Since you're working with specific animal images, it's logical to have at least part of the visualization take place in that creature's natural habitat.

5. Consider adding external stimulus that can make the pathworking more realistic. For example, if you have decided to use a waterfall backdrop, having a tape or CD playing the sounds of a waterfall softly behind you becomes an external cue to verify the internal landscape.

6. Ask yourself what challenges or obstacles should be placed between you and the goal (the exit point). For example, if your goal is continuing your education but money presently stands in your way, a pile of money guarded by a bear might become part of the path. In this case you'll have to figure out how to surmount that obstacle using the pathworking's imagery.

7. If you're working with a pathworking partner, determine if this individual will vocally guide you through the devised pattern, and possibly pose questions that help determine the unfolding landscape.

The idea of pathworking is relatively new for many readers. If you find any of the above seven points somewhat confusing or unclear, reading over the following sample pathworkings should help clarify the process. If you cannot get a pathworking partner to work with you, Granny suggests taping the progression for yourself leaving suitable pauses where noted in the text. The pauses are where you'll be watching, listening, or making a decision, so you need that time built in.

When working with a guide, make sure it's someone who can remain sensitive to your reactions throughout the pathworking. The internal landscape can (and frequently does) change for the pathworker from what was originally planned. The guide must know how to watch for signals and energy shifts that imply such changes and then respond accordingly (by pausing, by asking questions, or by presenting options).

Guides please note: If at any time the seeker chooses not to move forward on the path (stops, says no, or shows other types of discomfort) do not proceed. Ask if they would like to take a different path or return home, then honor that choice. There are times when we are not meant to walk a particular road; sometimes the road is too hard or too long. In either case, you need to trust the seeker's self-awareness in this matter.

Ugly Duckling

This pathworking encourages better self-images based on an old animal fable. Even the most adept wild witch has insecure moments and needs an occasional boost. This pathworking is designed to provide that upbeat energy.

You might want to have a handheld mirror ready for this activity, but it can be done without one. The person going through the path should prepare himself or herself through deep, rhythmic breathing and at least five minutes of deep meditation. When the guide notices the pathworker's breathing taking on a pattern similar to sleep, that's when the activity can begin.

Guide speaking: *Look into your mind's eye. As you search around the darkness, you will see several doors. One of them has an image of a rather scraggly duck on it. Go to that door* [pause]. *Are you there?* [If the seeker says "yes" then continue.] *This door leads to the world of self-images . . . everything that you think of yourself; all that you are and all you can become. Do you wish to go through the door?* [Wait for an affirmative response.]

Open it slowly and walk through. On the other side you're greeted by the duck whose picture was on the door. Duck Spirit is your guide here, for he knows what it is to not see oneself clearly. You're in a long hallway filled with mirrors on both sides. Duck Spirit reaches out his feathered wing offering to help you in this journey. Do you accept his help? [Pause for a reply.] *Good, then take the wing and follow to the first mirror.* [If the seeker is using a real mirror, place it in his or her hands at this juncture so he or she can look into it.]

    This is the mirror of the past. If you look at the duck beside you in it, he is no more than a misshapen egg in a nest. Now look at yourself. What negative images have you carried since your youth that are no longer true, realistic, or healthful? Look! [Pause and give the seeker time to think about all the images that come to the forefront of the inner mirror.] *You can release those images now. Do you wish to?* [Wait for an affirmative answer.] *Good! Then turn your back to that mirror and do not look back. Your past is always with you, but you need not cling to those things that do not help the present or build toward the future.*

    Duck Spirit moves you farther down the corridor. These are mirrors of the present. Duck appears exactly as he did at the outset of the path, but what about you? Now that you've released negative images from the past, has your perception changed? Also, ask yourself—what expectations do you have in the here and now? What are you doing for the sake of propriety, to fulfill others' image of you, to make yourself feel "good enough" "handsome enough," or "beautiful enough"... these, too, aren't healthy. [Pause for various images and feelings to manifest.] *Do you want to release yourself from present images that aren't truly helping you become happy and fulfilled?* [Pause for affirmative reply.] *Good. Then turn and walk the rest of the way down the hall with Duck Spirit. The present is still with you, but only those self images that are life affirming and supportive remain.* [Pause so the seeker can mentally move farther down the hall.]

    At last we come to the mirror of the future. As you look, it seems to shift and change, second by second. That is because your future isn't fixed. Life is, indeed, what you make it. Nonetheless, at your right you see Duck Spirit, now manifest as a beautiful, full-grown swan that glows with golden white light. It smiles gently at you and begins to sing. Listen to this song, for in it you will find healing and peace. [Pause for about 3 minutes—Guide: if you have any soft music that can be played at this juncture it helps the effect.]

    When Swan's song is over, the mirror disappears and becomes a simple door, just like the one by which you entered. Do not look back. Don't accept the negative energy you've released here back into your life. Only take the lessons... only take the song in your heart. Are you ready to return? [Wait until seeker says yes.] *Then open the door and slowly open your eyes.* [At this point the seeker may want to talk about his or her experience, or minimally record it somehow, to ponder in the days ahead.]

Swan Song

The ugly duckling turns into a swan at the end of the story. So what's all the squawking about swans? The myth of the song of the beautiful dying swan appears in classic Greek literature, which is how it became associated with the Muse. Swans were sacred to Apollo and Aphrodite; in Hindu myth Brahma rides a swan; the Celts believed these birds could shape shift; and in complimentary moments contemporaries of Shakespeare called him the Swan of Avon.

Just the Elementals

For this pathworking we're going to rely on the assistance of four animals, each one of which represents one element. As you traverse the sacred wheel of this pathworking, you'll gather lessons from each creature about its element.

I suggest that this pathworking take place in a sacred circle that includes four altars, each with elemental imagery. You may certainly choose other animals as representatives of any quarter besides those we provide here so long as their natural living environment is keyed to that element. In this case we've chosen Bear Spirit for earth, Bird Spirit (your choice of bird) for Air, Lizard Spirit for fire, and Fish Spirit (your choice of fish) for water.

The seeker should once again prepare for a while before the pathworking. In particular the seeker should be able to bring to mind images of the four elemental guardians in the activity. Additionally, it helps to have a small token for each element that you can hold when you reach that point on the path. These can be given to the guide or left within arm's reach.

Guide speaking: *Welcome to this circle . . . to this space between the worlds . . . the space between breaths, between sounds and silences. This is a magickal sacred place where you are safe, and where your mind can roam freely through the dimensions. Knowing this, what is your desire?* [Pause for the reply—the seeker should speak whatever is in his or her heart, particularly about what he or she wants to learn of the elements.]

As it is said, so let it be! Open the stage of your mind and see yourself in a circle of trees. You are in the middle. Your life, mind, and heart are the altar on which these lessons will be written. Will you welcome the four guardians of this space to join you in this quest? [Pause for reply.]

Come ancient ones—representatives of earth and air, fire and water. Welcome! As you look around the circle you notice images forming at the four quarters. An outline of a bear in the North, a bird in the East, a lizard in the South, a fish in the West. Of these four one will become wholly solid before the rest. Which is it? [Wait for seeker to reply.] *Go to that quarter and take the symbol of the element you've brought with you and give it to the Spirit.* [Pause.] *Now, sit and ask this creature your questions. Listen with an open mind and heart. It will fade from your view when it has imparted its lessons.* [Pause for about 5 minutes.]

Your first guide is done, three still await. What is the second animal to come fully into view? [Pause for answer.] *Go to that quarter and take the symbol of the element you've brought with you and give it to the Spirit.* [Pause.] *Now, sit and ask this creature your questions. Listen with an open mind and heart. It will fade from your view when it has imparted its lessons.* [Pause for about 5 minutes.]

Guide repeats this very same procedure two more times. When the last creature leaves, continue. *Take a moment and whisper words of thanks to the powers that have stood watch and helped you on this day in any way you wish. As you do, you'll notice the trees fade away, your breathing return to normal. Open your eyes when you feel ready.* [Encourage the seeker to write down his or her experiences for pondering later.]

Please remember that pathworking is a flexible process. If you think of it like the rough outlines of an energy-oriented coloring book to which you bring the crayons of imagination, you'll get the idea. At any point the path can take an unexpected twist or turn that leads to an equally unexpected result. Nonetheless, sometimes we must trust that our higher self, our animal guides, and Spirit know what we most need (even when we perhaps don't). Remain open to those nudges and leadings when they happen. Listen to the wild within.

Plants (*Trees, Flowers, etc.*)

I want death to find me planting my cabbages.   —Montaigne

Earlier in this book we talked a bit about gardening and herbalism, so why bring up plants again? Because gardening and herbalism doesn't fully cover the spectrum of the plant world, nor do they completely deal with the idea of plant spirit or having a plant as a totem or teacher. That's the purpose for which this heading was designed.

In Shamanic traditions each plant has its own medicine. Now, by *medicine* I do not simply mean something that heals, but also the plant's spiritual lessons and knowledge. In this setting various seeds are ritually planted, grown in sacred space, harvested by a priest/ess, and even consumed in ritual in an effort to internalize that medicine. The entire process becomes a sacrament that attunes the individual to the plant's spirit, and the Great Spirit by extension.

Now, while I can see this being difficult if you don't have a lot of space, no one said such efforts to attune yourself had to be grand. How about starting with just one small potted plant? Pick out some seeds, bless them, sow them in sacred space, chant and dance around the plant whenever you work magick, and as it grows meditate nearby. Keep a journal of anything you learn from the way the plant grows, how it seems to respond to music or light, and if you begin to sense when it needs water.

Communing with Plant Spirits

This activity is a simple meditation designed to help you grow more attuned to the spirit of a plant. You may need to repeat the meditation several times for solid results simply because we are animals. Learning to understand the signals from the plant kingdom is difficult, especially since humans have often pushed away instinct in favor of logic.

Sit with the plant before you. Place your hands within six inches of the leaves or flowers (so you're in contact with the plant's aura). Close your eyes and begin to breathe slowly and evenly, as with any other meditation. This time, however, focus your mind and senses on the plant. Listen. Extend your touch, hearing, smell, and even taste to the spiritual level. Does anything seem different? For example, if you find your mouth very dry suddenly—perhaps the plant needs water. Or, if you get a rush of heat, perhaps it's getting too much sunlight.

Typically the signals you get from plant spirits will be on this sensual or symbolic level. You might get fleeting images in your mind, but because the plant "mind" is so different from ours, symbolic interpretation is easiest. Make notes of your experiences throughout that plant's life and compare them to another plant of the same genus and species. You'll find some strong similarities but differences too. Plants and animals are just as unique as we are!

Whether or not you ever choose to harvest the plant is up to you. You will certainly have a better feel for how you might utilize it in your magick. If you do decide to go this route, follow the same pattern. Harvest it in sacred space, dry it on your altar, and continue to charge it with blessings and other positive energy. This way, from start to finish, you've honored that plant's spirit.

Oh, and don't forget to replace it! Whatever we take from the earth we should also attempt to diligently return. Balance and reciprocity are two key words in any wise person's book. When we lose respect for any part of nature there's a tendency to misuse it. For example, when plant substances are abused, people become addicted or poisoned. That's why Shamans tell us that if we forget thankful gestures the plant spirits will grow angry and their medicine no longer work for us. Granny agrees wholeheartedly.

Physical Spells

Take care of your body with steadfast fidelity. The soul must see through these eyes alone, and if they are dim, the whole world is clouded.

—GOETHE

Granny is constantly amazed at how many times people forget about the one spiritual tool they have with them all the time—their body! If we quickly review many early spells it's obvious our ancestors weren't forgetting that physical magick works very well. The large number of spells or banishings for the evil eye alone bears witness to this truth. But we should not stop with the eyes by any means.

Add physical positioning to spells and rituals. For example, sit near to the ground (or on the ground) when doing Earth magick. Move from a sitting to a standing position to increase energy during a ritual. When releasing a spell, point in the direction you want the energy to flow (much as you would a wand).

In visualizations, position your body to help you "see" more clearly. To illustrate, if I'm doing a visualization to better connect with my bee totem, I might flap my arms like wings and walk slowly around the room to get a feel for that motion. In my mind's eye I can visualize myself winged like my totem and celebrate that connection.

Yes, these are very simple things, but don't be fooled by that simplicity. If used with thoughtful intention they powerfully mirror your intention in the physical plane, which your body then remembers until the intention manifests itself. Patterning your body into the magick is also very healthy for your aura. It keeps it saturated with those spiritual vibrations that encourage growth, balance, assurance, and overall well-being.

Politics *(Political Correctness)*

> *Those who do not do politics will be done in by politics.*
> —FRENCH PROVERB

In Granny's opinion the words *political correctness* and *paganism* have no place in the same sentence. Political correctness has gone badly awry and actually wears away at the very freedoms we hoped it would help! Be that as it may politics and paganism *do* (or at least they should) mingle. We need to be strong advocates, and raise our voices about important issues. If we do nothing—then we have no reason to gripe! Without eyes to watch and voices to speak against things like the ever-shrinking distance between church and state, we could see some terrible losses to personal liberties, not to mention privacy.

Please know it's not my intention to turn this topic into a personal political agenda. I am not here to tell you what to support, or who, but rather to support something and someone! Granny doesn't buy into the belief that one person can't make a difference. You can, but you won't if you never try!

How? Get involved. Watch the ongoing media updates on www. witchvox.com, write your senators and congresspeople, vote! Send editorial letters to your local newspaper, stay informed and aware—then educate others! Log onto a public bulletin board so you can discuss issues with other people. Gather others who feel as you do together and start a petition. Whatever your choice—*action* is the key word. Do not simply think about an issue—ask yourself what you can do to support or fight against that issue.

And don't forget spiritual options. Pray for our leaders. Work rituals for global healing and peace. Cast spells to the wind for wisdom and insight among those who are behind the scenes influencing decisions. Put a candle on your altar as an ongoing light beacon to the world that shines with hope that we will, indeed, begin to learn from history and grow as a species.

I wouldn't normally even bring up this subject, but in recent years I've witnessed an alarming trend: people losing sight of what's happening in our local and global governments. While keeping up with everything is nearly impossible, keeping a thumb on the overall pulse is wise. When the figurative blood pressure gets too high or too low in arenas of personal interest you can act to defray the cause of that illness.

Two groups that I personally belong to, the ACLU (www.aclu.org) and Americans United for Separation of Church and State (www.au.org), are very helpful in monitoring those pulses. If you have access to the Internet you'll get regular updates from this type of organization (and often postal mail too). From that information, you can determine what to act on, trusting your heart and spirit to guide you.

I won't belabor this point further, but please take a moment to think about it. Our children's future is in our hands. Let us hope and pray to leave our space in better condition than when we came into it!

Poppets

If we are to change our world view, images have to change
—DAVID HOCKNEY

Poppets are among the oldest forms of sympathetic magick that also work hand in hand with the Law of Similars. Small representations (dolls usually) of a person or animal are created and then utilized in magick. The figurine's power comes from the symbolic connection between the poppet and what it represents, knowing that a symbol has all the same powers and energies in the sacred space as a real object.

To explain: the Law of Similars states that like causes or cures like. Thus, in early herbalism, a plant that looked like a heart might be tried as a cure for heart problems, or a yellow plant might be used for jaundice. Likewise, the Law of Sympathy states: That which seems alike, is alike. So, the use of poppets in magick begins to make a lot of sense. It's supported by two laws healers and mystics have depended upon for thousands of years.

Historically poppets were often used for curses, but we're obviously going to consider more positive applications. The media for your poppets can be nearly anything from potatoes and lemons to cloth or clay. One medium that I'd like to suggest, however, is origami (folded paper).

There are several beauties to this system. Not only are there a wide variety of paper colors, sizes, and shapes available (including metallics) but this is a recyclable spellcraft form! Choose the color of your paper according to the goal. Then go to www.origami.com and pick out a pattern that also reflects your goal. Note that you can write wishes on the paper, dab it with oils, attach pictures to it, etc., before you fold it up.

What happens to the poppet once it's created, depends heavily on your goal. If like affects like, you want the poppet's final condition to reflect the magick as manifested. For example, if you're making an image of a bad habit, you'd want to perhaps burn or bury the poppet to destroy the habit. If the poppet represents an unfulfilled hope, you might want to leave it on the altar to collect and transmit positive energy toward those ends. To send the poppet's energy outward, you can float it on a live water source, burn it and give the ashes to the winds, or carry it in your pocket like a charm!

By the way, if you're feeling really creative, it's fun to make your own origami paper because you can do so ritually, adding whatever colors and aromas you wish (use up leftover incense, scrap paper, glitter, etc.). There are several websites with fantastic instructions including:

hometown.aol.com/Ppreble2/paper.html
www.pioneerthinking.com/makingpaper.html
www.geocities.com/Heartland/Pointe/2357/paper.htm

Just remember that for origami your frames must be square or the folding methods will not work.

Practice

> *If you practice an art, be proud of it and make it proud of you... It may break your heart, but it will fill your heart before it breaks it; it will make you a person in your own right.*   —Maxwell Anderson

The Buddhists had it right when they said that the key to a truly enriching and successful spiritual life is threefold: practice, practice, practice! Nonetheless, in a fast food, drive-through world it's not a concept that's easily digested. Spiritual and magickal process is not something instantaneous. It requires ongoing trial and error—in other words, practice!

I share this with you for two reasons. First, sometimes we lose sight of the importance of our experimentation process. People get discouraged because they don't see shake-'n'-bake results from their magick, meditations, or whatever. Second, people who have been on this Path for years can start feeling overly confident and stop putting time into developing their Arts.

Let's tackle the novice first. Like any Art, you're not going to become the Leonardo of the magickal world in a few days, let alone a few years. And the success you experience will be heavily dependent on how much effort you put in. If you're weaving magickal thoughts and process into your daily life, you'll have far greater success than if you just dust off your Art for a monthly coven meeting. Find one part of your Art that you want to develop and give it your time and attention for at least a year. You don't have to forego everything else during that year, but let that *one* item be your focus. At the end of that period, you'll be able to gauge your growth substantively. Better still, magick is a cooperative Art. The skills you learn in one area often help you in all the rest!

And for us old-timers, how can we keep our Arts fresh? Well, by learning something new for one thing. When I found my practices stagnating, I studied Strega for a while. It gave form and fullness to my rather amorphous, and often spontaneous, approach. Similarly, when I felt like writing one more spell would drive me nuts, I took time off and worked on my meditative abilities. Switching gears keeps all of them from getting rusty!

I see magick and spirituality like an upward spiral. We move around the wheel developing and improving our abilities. During this process we reach plateaus, but the spiral still moves upward. What you once considered as being very skilled spellcraft (for example) can suddenly looks rather rudimentary in this new perspective. You now need to learn how to apply your Arts to the new person you're becoming every moment of every day! So keep the faith, and keep practicing!

Promises

A promise is a cloud; fulfillment is rain.   —ARAB PROVERB

Promises are far easier to make than to keep. Nonetheless, this witch is a woman of her word, and feels strongly that ethics demand we make every effort to fulfill our commitments. What are some of the magickal and spiritual means people used historically to help them in this arena?

Well, one interesting promise was the Slavic tradition of making an oath with the Earth bearing witness (typically a promise of land). People would place their hands on the soil and make a commitment and speak their promise. Alternatively they would exchange handfuls of dirt. The symbolic value here was the oath was unbreakable even in death, because the Earth will be around long after we die!

The Arabs often used salt as a binding tie in commitments because the salt is "pure" (or a purifier). Romans swore oaths to Zeus (sometimes smiting a pig at the same time to show what would happen if the promise was broken). Christians use the phrase "so help me God" similarly—um, without the pig, that is! And in medieval times meeting under the symbol of a rose acted as a promise of privacy and complete secrecy regarding any information exchanged.

Promise Token

In reviewing these examples, all of the components are still readily available and have good symbolism for our purposes. So why not make a promise amulet for yourself that includes rich soil, salt, and rose petals, then charge it by invoking a patron/ness Deity?

For example, one of the beings I call upon is Ea. So, the blessing may take this form:

> *Roses that my trust be true*
> *Salt that intentions honor me and you*
> *Soil in which the promise roots, we defend*
> *Ea to our promise, attend!*

Obviously you can change your words so they're more specific to the promise being made. Then each person should carry a bit of the mixture to remind them of their word.

Protection *(Proactive Magick)*

> *Your own safety is at stake when your neighbor's wall is ablaze.*
> —HORACE

The phrase *Forewarned is forearmed* has a lot in common with protective magick. In my opinion, it's far better to have safety zones in place all the time, and continually reinforce your wards than to wait until something happens and *then* work protective magick. By then it's damage control, not protection!

Protection needs to be comprehensive (above, below, around, within, without, and outstretching). I find it interesting when people come to me saying they think they're under a psychic attack, they've done protective magick, and it's not working. I go visit them, and discover they forgot to include windows, air ducts, chimneys, etc. Protection has to go over everything including *you*.

In all instances of safety spells, protective potions, rituals, etc., it's a good idea to spiritually cleanse things first. Why? Because if you don't first remove the negativity, for all intents and purposes you run the risk of sealing that negativity *inside* the bubble instead of putting it out. Thus, I recommend that you think multidimensionally when you work protective magick.

Once you finish spiritual housecleaning, you can consider what form you want the protective magick to take. Here's a list from various friends about what they do:

- Visualize images of white light all over your walls, ceilings, floors etc. You can use classical art for the imagery, but you can pattern it like a web, make mosaics, or whatever!

- Set up a semiformal sacred space using four elemental objects that can be called into action using simple trigger words.

- Bless the house right after doing weekly cleaning.

- Hang up garlic near the hearth. Toss one clove outside whenever there's a sense of danger.

- Put the image of your home, yourself, your loved ones, pets, and so forth into a protective spell box (lined in tinfoil and white natural cloth). Keep this in a safe place (on your altar is one option).

- Create house candles that you saturate with protective energies. Light them in every room of the house as needed.

- Hang blessed, charged sun catchers in every window (choose the colors and patterns to better represent the type of energy you want them to "filter out").

- Hang a multifaceted clear crystal in your windows so it can scatter rainbows of light all through the space (the light of hope and blessings).

As you can see from this list, your efforts need not be overly grand so long as they're consistent. People who live in urban environments will need to reinforce their shields more often than rural dwellers just because of sheer numbers. Nonetheless, in either setting, set yourself up on a schedule and work this in regularly so you always abide within sacred space.

Psychism

Intuition is the source of scientific knowledge. —ARISTOTLE

Just to clear up one huge misconception: Not all psychics are witches, and not all witches are psychic. With that caveat out of the way, I will say that I think everyone has psychic potential. The key is discovering that potential and waking it out of the latent stage and into an active role in our lives.

Most people call psychic twinges "gut instinct"—and really, go with that! It's a good place to begin. The more you listen to that inner drive, the more likely you are to discover how accurate it is. And at that juncture you can work on improving accuracy.

Treat psychic methods as you might a science. Try one for a specific period of time during which you log the results of your efforts. Write down every reading, your interpretation of the information you get, and so forth. At the end of that period (I recommend at least six months) go back and read over your materials. Next to each attempt, gauge the accuracy based on current circumstances. Do this again in another month, then in several months. You should begin to see whether that method is going to be effective for you.

TYPES OF PSYCHISM
- Automatism
- Telekenetics

TOOLS OF PSYCHISM
- Ouija boards
- Dowsing rods

TYPES OF PSYCHISM

- Psychokenesis
- Remote seeing
- Mediumship, channeling
- Object reading
- Telepathy
- Empathy

TOOLS OF PSYCHISM

- Pendulums
- Tarot decks
- Runes
- Crystal spheres
- Dreams
- Omens/signs

Some people have a tendency toward one particular "gift" while others find using a tool gives them the doorway to releasing their psychic self. Some nice things about tools are that they decrease the overall energy drain, give you something on which to focus, and come in a wide variety from which to choose. There are also a variety of plants and stones said to enhance or help us "tap" our psychic abilities. These include:

- Bay leaf (in dream pillows or incense)

- Celery seed, nutmeg, thyme (kitchen magick)

- Dandelion, marigold, rose (in salads or dried for charms, etc.)

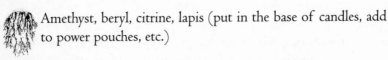 Amethyst, beryl, citrine, lapis (put in the base of candles, add to power pouches, etc.)

For more ideas and information on this topic, see Divination, earlier in this book.

Quiet

Meditate. Live purely. Be quiet. Do your work with mastery. Like the
moon, come out from behind the clouds! Shine. —BUDDHA

In our hurry-up world filled with noise one of the most important gifts
you can give yourself is some peace and quiet. In the moment between
breaths there is silence. Between this world and the next, there is a pause
of silence. In silence Spirit speaks (mostly because it's one of the few
opportunities in which the sacred can get our attention)!

Think of how you're barraged with noise even in your sleeping
hours. Honking horns, barking dogs, music. Now think back to the
last time everything around you was blissfully peaceful and still. What
was that moment like? Did you notice your tensions waning? I'm willing to bet you did. Silence acts like a salve to our very soul. Perhaps that
is why the Ute have a prayer that says:

Earth, teach me stillness.

That is a great prayer and it's one best offered outdoors, as far away
from human influences as possible. Yes there are many sounds in nature,
many songs, but there is also stillness.

I can't tell you exactly how much time to spend in silence because I am not you. I don't know how much stress exists in your life, how complex or busy it is. I do recommend that everyone take time for silence at least once a week if only for ten minutes. Get earplugs, turn off the phone, or hide in the bathroom if need be!

The practice of silence requires no particular posture, but I do recommend being still (the two kind of go together). Movement makes sound and also distracts the mind. Don't be surprised if you find yourself a little antsy at first. A lot of people report that finding quiet and being silent is just as difficult to learn as meditation. We have grown accustomed to our noise—but you will be quite surprised to discover many sounds in silences. In particular, this time reconnects you with personal biorhythms (breath, heartbeat).

You may also find that spiritual senses become far more acute because they're not being hit with so many outside influences. Consequently take a pen and paper, hush...and explore the silence.

Rattles

Beauty of style and harmony and grace and good rhythm depend on simplicity.　　　　　　　　　　　　　　　—Plato

Rattles have been an important religious and magickal tool since the time of the Egyptians. Most commonly they are used in ceremonies as background percussion, and the variety of rattles is impressive. Native Americans used birch bark rattles in funerary rites, Hawaiian hula dancers use feathered gourds, seventeenth century Turkish rulers proclaimed their power with crescent rattles, and Hopi Indians created them from turtle shells and baskets (often filled with seashells or stones). Other common materials used in making rattles include animal hides, claws and hooves, fruit shells, egg shells, various metals, and seeds.

The function of the rattle depended on the culture and the ritualistic setting in which it was used. In some cases it helped to mark a rite of passage. A rattle might be given to a young woman for dancing to mark her coming of age. In other cases it was protective, becoming what we sometimes call "rough noise" to scare away malicious spirits. Other rattles were used to inspire crops to grow, while still others motivated the dancers or chanters rhythm (also a very important ritualistic function since rhythm aids in shifting our awareness from the temporal into the eternal).

One beauty of rattles is that as long as you have a sense for keeping a beat, they are very easy to transport, most are relatively inexpensive, and they're pretty darn durable too. Before I was given a drum I took small egg shakers in my carry-on luggage to events so I could dance and rattle to spiral the fire's energy. In spellcraft and ritual I've found that shaking a rattle helps build energy (the faster and louder the sound, the closer you're getting to releasing that cone to where it's intended). But the usefulness of rattles doesn't stop there.

Consider meditation. If you use a rattle to mirror the beating of your heart you'll find your meditative state naturally deepening. From this point, let whatever inner beat you hear become part of what you're manifesting externally. In a group setting this often makes for very sweet grooves of rhythm where the All and the One blend harmoniously into purpose.

Better still, rattles can be made out of nearly anything. I've used a capped coffee mug, a food storage container, and even a plain paper bag that's been decorated with glitter or flowers and feathers and then filled with crystals, seeds, rice, or other noise-making items. When making something like this, try it first with one internal medium and see if you like the sound. If not, try another. You can also try blended mixtures to create a soundscape that's uniquely your own.

About the only caution I have regarding rattles is to be mindful when you're using them in conjunction with other instruments. High-end sounds that some rattles produce can drown out the drummers, who reflect the community heartbeat. So in settings like these you need to use the instruments in sensitivity with the All. Instead of being the largest tree, let the rattles blend gently and respectfully into the forest of sound that's being created.

Sadness

Not only is there a right to be happy, there is a duty to be happy. So much sadness exists in the world that we are all under obligation to contribute as much joy as lies within our powers. —JOHN S. BONNELL, D.D.

While one might wish that life were always happy, there is balance in all things. Granny knows that sadness sometimes threatens to drown us in its churning sea. This is also typically the time when we find our faith failing, and question many things. Worse still is that if this condition lingers too long it can lead to disease, apathy, and inactivity (as we know now, depression is a clinical issue and growing rapidly in our culture).

Banishing Blues

When you find yourself in this position, I suggest tackling the problem on two fronts. The first front is mental and spiritual. You need to change your way of looking at things and reclaim the reigns of control in your life. The minute you believe you can—*you can!* I often find that even a little spell, personal affirmation, or miniritual helps shake off some of the depression's weight and provides enough breathing space to actually get out and do something productive. Some of the components traditional to this type of magick include hawthorn flowers, lavender, marjoram, amethyst and chrysoprase. I suggest blending some of these together into an amulet not only to lift your mood, but also help keep your outlooks upbeat. An incantation suited to this task might be something like:

> *I've been feeling very bad*
> *My heart's been heavy, lonely and sad*
> *But my will and magick knows the way*
> *To lift my spirits, by night and day*
> *In these components this magick combines*
> *Peace of heart; peace of mind*

Place your tokens into something portable. Also, as you work your magick, or just before, consider putting on a piece of brightly colored clothing (pink or orange in particular bear the right vibrations), open the windows, and let in as much sunlight as possible. Darkness is frequently equated with sadness, and letting in light can provide the extra mental advantage to support your spiritual efforts. I also suggest doing some astral house cleaning so that your sacred space isn't holding in any negativity. Remember, your home is your haven, and you want it to be as positive as possible.

And by the way, it's okay to feel crummy sometimes. It's okay to let yourself have those "moments"—sadness and grief are part of our humanness. If you don't let them out, they can be very damaging. The key here is not letting those states become the focus of your life, or wallowing in them too long. I mention this because sometimes our community seems very impatient. When someone is having a bad day, we may perceive it as mere attention seeking or putting on a "poor me" attitude—when all that he or she may really need is a little time to work through it, and/or some support.

Self-Images and Self-Esteem

Your sacred space is where you can find yourself again and again.
—Joseph Campbell

It's interesting that even the most talented of people have self-doubts from time to time. Others, like myself, wake up one day realizing they're still suffering from teenaged angst (the you're-not-good-enough, beautiful-enough, successful-enough–type stuff). In part this comes from having unreasonable expectations, and in part from our society that constantly puts pressure on the individual through advertising and other media.

I've always been fond of the idea that people become truly beautiful as they get older, because of what's developed within. That wisdom and insight is a beauty that cannot be touched by time or perspectives. Nonetheless, our world puts a lot of stock in outward appearances and performance. How does a spiritually mindful person balance out these pressures with the inner life? Not an easy question, and it's one with which I often grapple too. Here's one activity that you may find useful:

Assurance Affirmations

Since a great deal of our self-image begins in our own mirrors, I suggest trying this activity in front of whatever mirror you use most often. You will need to determine in what area of your life you need more confidence, and then write one or two affirmations (positive statements) that support that goal. An affirmation begins traditionally with the words I *am*, because the phrase nurtures individuality and sense of Being. Alternatively, "I can" works.

Take the example of external images. Phrases like:

- I am beautiful.

- I am a shining spirit.

- I am the light of magick.

- I am God (or Goddess).

- I am the master of my fate.

- I am whole within and without.

- I am significant and important.

- I can make a difference.

- I can control my destiny.

support your goal of improving self-image. These phrases should be repeated several times every morning (at the outset of your day so as to set the tone). Say them out loud as you look in the mirror. Let your voice naturally rise with an air of authority. Say it! Hear it! Believe in the truth of your words!

Continue this same set of phrases until you see significant transformations in those perspectives. Then you can go on to work in another area of your life.

I know it might be tempting to try to focus on several sore spots at the same time, but don't unless it's an emergency. Typically if you divide your attention too much, it takes a lot longer and you could find yourself growing quickly discouraged (the very opposite of the goal at hand!). Also realize that if your self-image or confidence has been damaged over a very long time, it will likely take a longer time for you to see some success from this effort.

Signs and Omens

The trouble with our age is all signposts and no destination.
—Louis Kronenberger

In humankind's earliest history, the most prevalent type of divination used omens and signs. In animistic belief systems all things in nature (the wind, creatures, rains, etc.) were thought to have indwelling spirits. If you watched those Powers closely, you could discern messages from them. Typically someone who became very adept at omen observation and interpretation (cause and effect) became a spiritual leader—a Shaman, if you will.

Similarly where omens leave off, signs begin. A sign is defined as anything that provides an indication of something yet to come. Signs have a slightly broader basis for interpretation, therefore, as they can include things outside of nature and her citizens like overhearing a snippet of information in a conversation, meeting people unexpectedly, and dreams. Taking this one step further I'd add technological oddities to this list, like the clock that keeps stopping at a specific time (even after being fixed).

I covered some ideas along these lines in the Divination section earlier in this book; however, Granny is also a believer in coincidence. While the patterns of our lives often evoke signs and omens that help us either break or keep that pattern, sometimes proverbial "shit" does happen! Humans have free will, and we cannot control every minute aspect of our environment or our reality (and to be honest, I'm not sure we'd be responsible with it if we had such control). I think the important thing is delineating what is an actual sign or omen, and what is life simply happening in your vicinity. (Or as I like to say "Sometimes a blade of grass is just a blade of grass!")

Hints of Omens and Signs

How do you go about determining one versus the other? Now, that's a great question. Personally I have several ways of answering it. First, I ask myself if the situation that just happened has any bearing on something I've been pondering deeply, or a connection to any magick I've been working. If it does, that's a pretty good indicator that I should consider further. This comes under the heading of "Why is this happening to me, and did I bring it about?"

Second, I think back to see if this particular set of circumstances seems cyclical or repetitive. If it happens at least three times—all kinds of whistles and bells go off in my mind. After all, as the saying goes, *three is a charm!* Additionally, I've noticed that when the Universe is trying to get our attention, it usually gives us more than one chance to catch the clue. In other words, "Why is this happening yet again?" Sometimes it's a matter of not taking steps to break a cycle, and in other cases it's a gentle nudge to *do something.*

Third, I consider what was (or is) happening all around me at that moment (i.e., where am I and what's the scoop). For example, if I get caught in a rainstorm that's no big deal (that's normal life happening). If the rainstorm seems centered on just me, or seems to follow me—that's a little different. I remember one time while traveling in Scotland the rain and dreary skies were everywhere. Nonetheless, each time we entered a town, the sun would peek through the clouds. I took that as a sign of welcome and blessings because it happened consistently for an entire week!

Generally speaking if you use these three touchstones you'll be less likely to jump at every shadow as having great import. Not everything in life has to have deep, spiritual meaning. Just make sure you're paying attention to the things that do!

Sleep

*The amount of sleep required by the average person is about five minutes
more.* —MAX KAUFFMANN

There are days that I would give nearly anything for a decent nap or a
full night's sleep. Besides having children and often finding myself too
wound up to rest properly, I have physical aches and pains and outside
noises with which to contend. These "mommy" ears pick up everything! I know, too, that I am not alone.

Sleep is very important in our spiritual and mundane lives. We need
to be properly rested for the self to be truly whole and capable of magick. Additionally, our dreamtime can be very telling (see Dreams). But
it's hard to dream if you can't even get through an hour or two of sleep!
So what does Granny recommend? Well for starters meditation (covered herein under Meditation). This is a very relaxing activity and one
that can naturally carry you off into a deep, restful sleep. It's also excellent as a proverbial "power nap" when you're short on time.

Sleepy-Time Tea

Second, look to our Cunning Folk herbalists for assistance. Make
yourself a presleep tea from chamomile, catnip, valerian, mint, lavender,
or thyme (or a blend). One word of warning—valerian has a nasty
aroma, so you'll want to cover it up with something else! Stir the tea
clockwise with whatever additives (honey, lemon, etc.) you wish, adding
an incantation like:

> *When taken to my lips*
> *Peaceful sleep in every sip*
> *This magick brew, quaffed deep*
> *Brings to me a night of sleep!*

Moonstone Slumber

Third, try placing four moonstones around your bed—one at each of the four sides. You can energize these stones by saying:

> *Four by four, side by side*
> *In this room rest abides*
> *Within, without and all around*
> *Gentle rest and sleep abound*

You can repeat this incantation quietly to yourself as you meditate or before trying to sleep.

Spellcraft

Who lies beneath your spell.   —LAURENCE HOPE

It is nearly impossible to think of Cunning Folk and witches without a healthy dose of spells in their arsenal. Nonetheless, I get dozens of letters every year from people asking if it's "okay" for them to create their own spells, and if so how they should go about it. To ease the process, I've written two books you may find useful. One is *Magick Made Easy*, which is set up by components, and the other is *Spinning Spells—Weaving Wonders*, which is an alphabetical compendium of sample spells to use or adapt.

However, since this is a book of advice, I'm going to put my two cents in on the subject here, too. First, magick and spellcraft are a birthright. You need not have any particular aptitude so long as you're willing to study and get to know how the process works. In particular you need to understand how the various parts and ingredients of a spell get combined and why.

In spellcraft, symbolism and focus make or break the energy. However you put together your spell needs to reflect its goal and to build energy in a natural way. All the component parts must match that goal, and make sense to you, and you need to be in the right frame of mind to work the magick (focus). Ah, but let me back up a moment.

Steps for Constructing a Spell

1. Consider the goal in as much detail as possible.

2. Boil down that goal to words, symbols and movements that are easily used in the sacred space.

3. Use the words for invocations, prayers, or incantations.

4. Use the symbols as components of focal points.

5. Put everything together in a progressive form (so as to raise energy). Take care that this form mirrors the goal.

6. Cast the spell (making note of anything that seemed really good or really off).

7. Make notes of the results.

Let's talk about this process. You need to ask yourself what your goal is and what items you have in and around the house that match that goal (by their color, scent, shape, common usage, etc.). Don't forget that your own body can become a spell component or symbol, and that even just a few items properly chosen can create potent magick.

Next, ask yourself what needs to happen to the components of the spell. For example, in many banishings the components disappear by fire, water, or another process to emphasize the dispersal of energy. Finally, ask yourself when to work the spell, and where. I don't often use fire-oriented magick in the house because of pets and children, nor do I work with potential allergens in an enclosed space. Also, you want to avoid distractions—focus is important.

All that remains now is to give the process a fair try. If you find that something doesn't feel right as you move through the spell, make note of it and try again with appropriate modifications. Spellcraft is like any other magickal process—trial and error do refine it, and create more and more successful results. Transfer those spells that feel really good, and from which you get solid manifestation, into your personal Book of Shadows for future reference.

Superstition *(Tradition)*

> *Who can define the boundary line between the superstition of yesterday and the scientific fact of tomorrow?*   —GARRETT FORT

Anyone who reads my books knows that I depend heavily on folklore, superstitions, and the traditions of "common" people (who were anything but common!). People ask me frequently why I value these so much, let alone rely on things that seem rather quaint and out of date. The first response to this inquiry is that just because something is "old" doesn't mean it has no function in the modern world. In fact, so many of our symbols and processes come from the traditions of our Ancestors, that it's rather silly to think that "modern magick" is truly "modern" (kind of like New Age being a misnomer).

Folklore and myth are part of what binds any group of people together. In those stories and actions, people find lessons, ethical constructs, and ideas for daily living. Superstitions also have very strong binding ties, because most of them came about via thorough observations and then passing along the conclusions from generation to generation (with minor variations). Where folklore and myth have commonality among a people, superstitions are a little more tribal (like tossing salt over your shoulder because Grandpa did). Thus, I've used superstitions that have magickal elements and that I find meaningful as a way of communicating to a "Tribe" of people—*you!*

I also find that folklore and superstition are, by nature, very simple, which makes them marvelously adaptable for our busy world. We have the symbolic value that empowers them, the fact that they're familiar to us (making them comfortable) and nearly every component of superstitions comes from everyday life (availability). Better still, since these traditions have been followed and trusted for hundreds (sometimes thousands) of years, by a great many people, there's a lot of cumulative energy there to tap.

Obviously, we have to tweak and adapt some beliefs so they mirror the human process and progress. We have a great deal more scientific knowledge today, making some of the original approaches inappropriate. For example, while blood was often used in spellcraft because it was very personal and symbolized life, we know the dangers of so doing today. So, we substitute red items—still the color of life and energy, but a much safer and healthier option.

I encourage you therefore to dig around in your familial or cultural superstitions and lore and see what gems you may find there. If you read something and go "Wow, that was a neat idea"—take a second look and see if you can't apply the concept to your workings. And don't be afraid to get creative here! Someone, somewhere had to be the first to pick a component for a spell or ritual, or the wording of an incantation. You're doing the same exact thing, but allowing folk beliefs to create the foundation for you. A little work, and a lot of fun!

Sympathy and Similars

*Nothing in the world is single; All things by law divine In one spirit mix
and mingle.*   —PERCY SHELLEY

Two important principles to understand (especially for spellcraft) are
the Laws of Sympathy and Similars. Beginning with Sympathy, this law
basically states that those things that seem alike *are* alike in a sacred
context. This means that any symbolic item, when used correctly, becomes what it represents in the magickal space, or acts upon what it
represents in the spiritual sense. To provide some examples of using
this idea to your advantage, let's say you come across an old spell that
calls for blood as a component. Now, most modern practitioners
would never consider such a thing, but using the law of sympathy we
can use any red liquid instead.

Going one step further, the Law of Sympathy also states that as the
unity of form increases, the connection between any two objects
strengthens. This, in turn, makes that form more suited to the channeling of magic. If you return to read the section on image magick and
poppets, their use now makes perfect sense because the shape and dec-
oration of that poppet reflected its connection to that which it represented. In short, the object and that which it represents become part of
a cooperative during magick that allows the object to act upon the re-
cipient even over distances.

The second principle is the Law of Similars. Now, you'll quickly notice that it's difficult to separate the two as they've got strong corollaries. In the Law of Similars like is said to cure (or affect) like. In other
words, the patterns in nature act as clues, showing us how to utilize the
Earth's treasures. In particular this law was applied to Homeopathy,
but Granny feels it has very strong applications in crafting our magick
too. For example, if you find a crystal that bears the shape of a heart
and/or a reddish hue, the Law of Similars would indicate that it would

be good to use that as part of a charm or spell for emotional issues. Likewise, returning to the poppets we've been talking about, the way you decorate the poppet mirrors the person or animal toward whom your energy is being directed. That's because the two look alike, thereby increasing Sympathy! Better still, your actions toward the poppet here help to shape the energy. Just like the stone's pattern implied its purpose, now you're patterning the magick!

As you read over various books on the magickal arts you'll see these two concepts appear again and again. They remind us of how very important symbols are to our Craft. Choose yours with these principles in mind.

Teachers and Guides

Teachers open the door, but you must enter by yourself.

—CHINESE PROVERB

As I travel, read my mail, and scan various magickal newsgroups it's very common for at least one person, if not several, to come to Granny seeking a teacher. And while I take on very few personal students due to time constraints, I do understand the thirst to learn. When I first entered neo-Paganism there were very few teachers who came forward offering aid. To those who did I owe a debt of gratitude.

So how exactly do I answer these requests? Well, first of all I tell them (and now you) that you must be your own teacher and guide before you can find the "right" person to help you on any spiritual Path. This is very important. It helps avoid teaching shams and ego trips. If you already trust your instincts, and are motivating yourself to learn, you'll be far less likely to rush blindly into any self-proclaimed teacher's proverbial pool without checking for water!

It's often said that a teacher appears when the student is ready, and true to form this is rarely convenient timing! Patience is truly a virtue in this particular arena. In fact, many times those who end up being our best teachers and guides never even call themselves by that title. They simply say or do something that transforms our way of thinking and BE-ing, without anybody else knowing a thing about it!

In a more formalized setting, when you do think you've found a teacher it's very important to ask yourself if that person has the qualities you'd expect from any *good*, ethical instructor. In particular:

- Does he or she have a vision for where you're headed spiritually, and is that vision honored?

- Does he or she inspire you to think and do for yourself?

- Does he or she have any type of accreditation or formal training in this specific path (i.e., do they share from what they live daily—are they walking the walk)?

- Does he or she have other students who speak highly of what they've learned thus far?

- Does he or she respect your personal growth pace? (Each student has a specific pace at which it's possible to learn. Spirituality cannot be hurried for convenience sake.)

- Does he or she release students without negativity if they find they've taken the wrong Path? Beware of overly controlling teachers!

- Does he or she keep the focus on you (as opposed to trying to become a guru of sorts)?

- Does he or she offer time during which you can get counseling or other assistance (i.e., is this person reasonably available)?

Please remember to carefully examine the answers to questions like these before entering into a student-teacher relationship. This is a commitment on both people's parts, one that takes time and energy. You want to invest that time and energy in someone that doesn't simply mirror what you already know, but stretches you to new places and new ways of thinking. And like any exercise, that stretching needs proper preparation and pacing.

Techno Magick

Our imagination always outpaces our technology. The gap between the two is the distance the creative spark must jump in order to ignite our forward momentum.   —Dr. Jason Ohler

People sometimes laugh at the idea that technology can be used in spiritual practices. I am not among them. When we consider that yesterday's magick has become modern reality (especially in technology), it seems perfectly fitting that technological items become part of our Craft. This is also one way in which we keep things moving forward progressively, so that our magick doesn't become stale and outmoded.

While I appreciate tradition and all it offers us, Granny figures that if our ancestors had had microwaves and lighters available they would have used them (much as they did anything else that was handy, meaningful, and functional). Also, we must consider the impact these items have had on both our conscious and subconscious minds. It's hard to think of a space shuttle without thinking of adventure or exploration, for example (and also potential danger). It's hard to see a computer without thinking about communication. Thus, modern items are making a mark upon our awareness, one that magick can honor and utilize.

To begin the process of changing your perspectives about man-made items keep two words in mind: *potential* and *possibilities.* Also recognize that everything in this world has an astral presence. The way in which an item is utilized in day-to-day life provides its underlying thematic possibilities in that realm. For example, since we use microwaves to speed up our food-making process, there's no reason not to use this item similarly to "speed up" the manifestation of our magick. That personal meaning is what gives nonliving matter potential in the sacred space. We have a strong mental and emotional connection to the symbolic value.

One excellent example of this connection comes when we use a blank TV or computer screen as a scrying implement. Many people are unable to scry using a flat black mirror or a crystal, but experience success with the TV and computer surface. Why? Because our mind is already programmed to expect images to appear on those surfaces as if by magick! Add a little methodology to that expectation and you're bound to have a greater degree of success.

So I encourage you to go through your home and office space and look at it differently. Think about those things that have emerged even in the past fifty years and become an integral part of our daily reality. Make a list of them, then next to each write down the potentials and possibilities. My list includes things like:

- Memory chips—combine with rosemary oil to improve recollection

- Freezer—for cooling emotions or halting specific types of energy

- Countertop grill—alternative fire circle energy or hearth energy

- Yard and garden sprinkler—alternative asperger (that even goes clockwise)

- Superglue—security, stability, longevity

- DVDs and CDs (unusable)—make into Yule ornaments, paint with symbols, and put on a wheel for moving magick or prayers around in the direction most needed

- Bubble wrap—protection and safety spells (good combined with poppets

Even as a medieval monk recommended: See all things as possible implements of your sacred altar and your life will never quite be the same again.

Tools of the Trade

Tools arm the man.   —NOVALIS

From poppets and pendulums to candles and crystals, there are some other items besides herbs that are indispensable to a truly wise witch's kit, not the least of which is two willing hands and a loving heart. Even as I sit in front of my computer, I see dozens of potential tools for my craft, including paperclips, glue, stamps, business cards, thread, and children's toys! If you've never thought of such items as potential magickal tools, my challenge to you is to do so!

Right now take a pad and paper and walk around your living space. Write down a bunch of things you have lying around or use regularly, but never think much about (at least three). Three items from my list today are:

- Theme buttons (one that says: There are more of us than you think)

- Staple puller

- Marbles (various colors)

Now, next to each of those items make note of how they might be used in magick. Think out of the box here! Returning to my list, theme buttons can become part of power pouches or magickal cloaks that are blessed with the energy that the button represents. Mine is ideal for community magick or growth. What about the staple puller? Well, I'd probably use that when I need to find out the component pieces of a situation (take it apart) or when disassembling (banishing) energy—in this case literally yanking out the problem. Finally, I like the idea of using marbles to support the conscious, rational mind (based on the rather humorous saying "losing my marbles").

While these examples may seem a bit humorous and pun laden, don't forget that there is power in humor and puns (in fact, I'd love to write about pun magick some day!). Puns require a high level of intelligence to appreciate the twists and turns of words (especially in other languages), and humor is just good for you. If you allow these, along with simple corollaries to drive the way you apply emerging symbols—you won't go wrong. The best application is the one that makes sense in your reality.

Travel

The travel writer seeks the world we have lost.

—Alexander Cockburn

I have often joked that my dream was to have a huge yard in which I could mow the words "free parking" so that they could be seen by extraterrestrial visitors and I could hitch a ride, but in my heart that's not wholly a joke. Granny is a bit of a Gypsy by nature—who would travel the globe five times over if time and money allowed. And in looking at our world, we are truly a community of travelers. Some go from home to work, others from home to abroad, and others still from home to space.

As someone who travels (on average) about twenty-four times a year, I feel better when I have a little magick in my back pocket for protection and to avoid red tape. Of course, this amulet needs to reflect the type of transportation. I have one for my car and one for flying.

Car Charm

Take a little toy car, either one that looks like your vehicle, or a white one (for protection). Dab this with a protective oil (any type you wish). Visualize it filled with white light energy until it glows brightly in your mind's eye. As you do, add a verbal charm like:

> As the wheels go round, safety abounds
> When the ignition starts, smooth travel impart
> Near and far, protect my car

Put this in your glove compartment, recharging it after you've had any close calls on the road.

Airplane Charm

As with the car charm, use a toy airplane for this amulet. The visual representation of your mode of transportation helps support the spell in the same way that a poppet does (see also the entry "Poppet"). The process is essentially the same but for the verbal element, which might take this form:

> Powers of Air, bring me skies FAIR
> When I travel by plane, bring me safely home again
> Where delays are faced, all troubles erase
> Powers of Wind—this spell begins!

Tuck this in your carry-on luggage.

Victory *(Success)*

Success is that old ABC - ability, breaks and courage.

—CHARLES LUCKMAN

The power to overcome, the chance to succeed, the ever thirsty human soul that reaches ever higher...these are part of our experience on this planet. One of the most important gifts anyone can give himself or herself is a sense of hope—the sense that when you truly want to succeed, you can. Now, balancing that statement, this awareness shouldn't be based in overly ambitious goals. You need to be somewhat realistic.

To explain by example, as a child I wanted to be a successful astronaut, but unless I was willing to study higher sciences that goal would never be reached. I found those sciences overwhelming, so the victory there wasn't realized. Did I do anything wrong? Absolutely not. I tried, then realized that the Path was simply not right for me. So when you're thinking about magick for victory, I encourage you to also consider that success has many forms (including sometimes a momentary failure that teaches something necessary for future success). There are times to fight the good fight. There are also times to pause or retreat. There are times to overcome. Wisdom comes in knowing which is which.

Attainment Amulet

When you know you're going to need a little more fortitude and backbone with which to achieve a victory, make this amulet and keep it with you until the situation resolves. Gather a piece of amazonite, ginger-root, and cinnamon stick together with a blue, gold, or red pouch in which to house them. I think of blue and gold as victorious colors because they represent first place. Red also has strong victorious overtones, so choose the one that makes the most sense to you.

I suggest creating the amulet at the noon hour (sunlight has strong energies for success). Add a prayer or incantation like:

> *Amazonite for victory and might*
> *Ginger pure, for success that's assured*
> *Cinnamon stick—bring victory quick!*

Place these items in the pouch. When you've achieved your goal, grind up the ginger and cinnamon for supportive incense to keep that trend going.

Surpassing Potion

If you'd like something to help you internalize energies for overcoming, try this potion. To a base of orange juice (for healthy outlooks), add just a hint of ginger and cinnamon. Stir clockwise and use the same incantation only rework the first line to say: *Orange juice—success produce,* or something similar. Drink expectantly.

Visualization

*We are more than the sum of our knowledge, we are the products of our
imagination.*   —Ancient proverb

Visualization is the art of mindful imagining and it's typically combined with meditation. The first step in this process is choosing the
right images for the focus at hand. Please know that the image(s) need
not be complex. I suggest keeping things as simple as possible, especially for people who have trouble conjuring up pictures in the blank
slate of a quiet mind. In fact, one, well-utilized symbol can be just as
powerful as a complex visualization that follows a progression toward
your goal.

The key here is using the visualization form that works best for you.
If you're a step-by-step type person, you'll likely respond more positively to step-by-step visualizations that lead to a logical cycle fulfillment. If you're someone that's strongly impacted by *one* image or
atmosphere, then keeping the visualization simple makes sense.

In determining the form of your visualization, ask yourself again—
what am I trying to accomplish here? What images will best support
that goal? Find an image you can conceptualize easily or one that you
can memorize from a picture that then supports that goal.

Most important, don't fully depend on books of symbolism in your
decision-making process. Choose an image that makes sense to you. For
example, if you've had trouble getting yourself moving on a specific
project, the horse is a good choice of animal. But what exactly should
the horse be doing in this visualization? My suggestion would be seeing
yourself mounting the horse (getting "on the ball") and riding it toward the project's completion. The mental impact of taking up those
reins shouldn't be overlooked in this illustration.

Some solidly conceptualized animal visualizations that you can
adapt or try as they are follow.

The Butterfly of Change

Use this visualization to help make specific changes in your life. In this case the butterfly's natural life cycle from caterpillar to winged beauty becomes the catalyst for your own transformation.

Begin by getting comfortable. You may find this visualization easier if you stand, leaning against a wall throughout it. Take three deep, cleansing breaths in through your nose and out through your mouth. Now, starting at the tip of your toes, relax. Wiggle your toes a bit, and consciously let go of any negative or stressful energy there. When you feel them getting comfortable, visualize a beautiful little monarch butterfly coming into the room. This creature is not of flesh, but spirit, and it carries a silvery thread. Welcome it in any manner with which you feel comfortable, noticing that as it flies, it encloses your feet in a transformative cocoon.

Continue repeating this process upward through your body following the pattern of releasing tension and the butterfly increasing the size of the cocoon. Finish at the top of your head. As you close that last spot it becomes very still and dark within your space, but it also feels very safe. In this moment know that you can simply *be*. Here you are outside of worlds, outside of self. There's only you and Spirit. Take a few moments to ponder all that you have done and who you've become up to this point in your life.

Next, verbally affirm whatever changes you wish to make within this nurturing womb. Try to phrase this as if it were already accomplished (for example, rather than using the phrase "I will be _____" say I *am* _____. This helps with the manifestation process). Start out whispering, but let your voice naturally grow with the energy you're creating.

As your voice gets louder you'll notice a light breaking through from above your head. It's the butterfly again, bringing only the radiance of Spirit on its wings. The color of light will differ according to the kind of transformation on which you're focused. For example, healing transformations often appear as sprout-green in color. This light is warm and welcoming. It swirls around and around, washing over you, and you sense tingling everywhere. Eventually the intensity of the light-power explodes the cocoon outward and you see yourself as a human butter-fly.

Look at your wings and the colors and patterns there. Make a mental note of this, as it could prove very insightful later. Now, you like to go with these new wings? Do you need to overcome a barrier? Fly over it! Do you need new perspectives? Let your wings lift you! The old cocoon is gone as are those parts of self that are no longer productive. You feel as light as a feather—so fly. The butterfly spirit will join you.

Enjoy this feeling as long as you like. When you feel that you're finished, visualize your wings retracting into your body very slowly. Focus on the center of your stomach and begin really experiencing gravity. Thank the Butterfly Spirit for its help and bid it farewell. Let your breathing return to normal, knowing that the changes you've made will always be with you—your wings are still within. Make notes of your experiences in a meditation journal and consider what messages (if any) were in the colors and patterns in your wings. For example, yellow wings patterned with concentric circles might represent a new communicative skill emerging, whereas red ones with an upward pointing triangle speak of a connection with fire energies.

Dog Meditation/Visualization

Try this meditation when you feel your devotion and diligence waning. In this case, you'll be calling on the Dog Spirit for its faithful energies so you can "keep on, keepin' on."

If you're a dog owner, it can be very helpful to have your dog in your lap or lying on the floor nearby when you enact this visualization. Their warm, loving energy will become a natural helpmate to this process.

Begin as before by getting comfortable. In your mind's eye create an image of the person or situation toward which you need to direct your attention. This should appear realistically in the distance, somewhat like being at a drive-in theater.

Once that imagery is distinct, redirect your attention to the area just behind you. From a short ways away a friendly dog begins to approach. It doesn't rush, bark, or act odd. In fact, it seems wholly in its environment and recognizes you. Call to the dog using your thoughts. Welcome its energy.

Now, in the visualization bed down so that you're on the same level as the dog (remember you're welcoming it as a ally and a spiritual helpmate—meaning equality is important). In your own words, tell Dog Spirit what you need. Don't speak to it like a child; speak respectfully. Also picture your need since animal spirits often respond empathically.

At some point in this communication process the dog will offer you his or her paw (as if to shake hands). Accept it—this is the gift of energy that you've needed. Feel the flow from the animal spirit to you as it flows from your hand to your heart. Stay like that with Dog Spirit for as long as you feel comfortable. Listen if he or she has a message for you. When it's time to break that connection, Spirit will give you some kind of indication. At this point, don't tarry. Thank Dog Spirit and let it go on its way.

While the dog returns along the path by which it came, turn your sights back to the portrait you created. Call up the energy shared with you by Dog Spirit and promise yourself to focus that faithfulness on the task before you. Feel the energy reach from you to that portrait and connect you to it. Leave that connection firmly in place until your responsibilities here have finished (this means the line of energy stays on the astral level even after the meditation ends).

Return to normal levels of awareness and make notes of your experiences.

Overcoming Obstacles

Use this visualization to discover the reason for an obstacle in your life, and then surmount it by going under or around the wall!

Find a picture of a mole and study it for a few minutes before starting this meditation. As with the first meditation, get comfortable. This time we recommend being in direct contact with the Earth (like sitting on the grass) or as close as possible (perhaps sitting on the ground floor of your home).

Next, breathe deeply and visualize yourself as you sit right now. Notice every detail of your body. As you focus on various parts, let that part slowly grow low-pile fur, like that of the mole. Once the fur is grown begin imagining yourself growing smaller, and your feet and hands becoming as the mole's paws. Take your time, but throughout this process focus on becoming a determined earth-digging creature.

When you finally transform completely, see yourself in an outdoor location amid rich, loose soil. In the middle of the soil, spanning from one edge of your field of vision to the other, is an obstacle or wall. Name that wall according to your present difficulties. If, for example, you feel someone isn't being truthful, name the wall deception then proceed to dig under or around that wall to literally "dig up the dirt" and bring it into the open. Or name the wall "red tape" then dig all the way under the wall to either bring the wall down or put yourself neatly on the other side of it.

At the end of the digging process, let yourself transform back into human form. Grab a bit of the imaginary dirt and put it in your pocket. This represents taking that victorious energy with you as you emerge from the meditation. Let your breathing and focus return to normal, and make notes of your experience.

By the way, it's very important during these or any other visualizations to remember your purpose and exactly what your actions represent. Magickally speaking, this creates supportive energy for those goals in your spirit and aura, which you then carry into real life. Nonetheless, it won't happen without diligent focus and real effort on a mundane level.

Wisdom

Wisdom outweighs strength.   —AFRICAN PROVERB

What would the *Witch's Book of Wisdom* be without an entry on wisdom?

By dictionary definition wisdom is directly tied to our knowledge—it is, in fact, the best possible use and application for that knowledge. So, on this level we can consider wisdom a function of the conscious realm. Nonetheless, Granny feels that the intuitive self has a role to play here too—namely when spiritual or emotional issues come into play, or when we have to make a best guess as to what constitutes "for the good of all."

Some of the traditional components witches have utilized for wisdom include:

- Coral
- Sodalite
- Sage
- Fig
- Jade
- Sugilite
- Peach
- Mulberry

Some fun trivia —the mulberry gained its reputation because it was sacred to Minerva, while Peaches were associated with a Chinese folk heroine who became immortal by eating this fruit. So, blending these two would provide long-lasting wisdom (rather than letting good lessons flit away). Jade is favored for images of the Buddha because of its associations with wise energies, Sidhartha meditated beneath a fig tree, and coral became connected with wisdom because it's linked with the sea (and the moon), and with all their elemental insight.

Putting these components together, you might eat a fresh peach before meditating, and then place a piece of jade or sodalite on your third eye during the meditation. This opens the pathways for higher wisdom. Or, you can carry sage leaves and burn or crumble them when you need insights quickly. Dried figs also make a good portable wisdom charm that you can snack on when you want your words to be sagacious.

Wisdom's color is typically blue or purple. Blue has more mundane connotations, while purple reflects spiritual wisdom. Dress in these hues or add accents in your sacred space to support your efforts.

Wishes

Many of us spend half our time wishing for things we could have if we didn't spend half our time wishing. —Alexander Woollcott

Wish magic is one of the favorite items in Granny's bag of goodies. Everyone wishes. If you've blown out candles on a birthday cake or tossed a coin in a fountain, you've practiced a kind of wish magic that's very ancient, and still holds tremendous merit today because it's so familiar and user friendly. Better still, it's a custom about which no one seems to think twice. This subconscious acceptance of it provides a lot of manifestation power.

Throughout the world there are so many ways of wishing. The ones most important to you, however, are those with which you've grown up, or learned in your life and still utilize. You can apply the wishing tradition in its exact form, and simply include additional magickal methods or components to the process. For example, people toss coins in wells with a wish (often for prosperity). What about floating rose petals on flowing waters as a wish for love? Similar approach, but the symbolism has changed to reflect the goal.

Recycling and Wishing

This activity is fun for children and adults alike. Take some paper that has one side blank. Cut it into 1-inch wide strips, on which you write your wishes. To this add watercolor designs, aromatic oils, or anything else that symbolizes your desire. Now, roll a glue stick down the length of the paper saying:

> *Roll of wishes, sealed with glue*
> *By my will, my wishes come true!*

Take a wooden skewer (like those for the grill) and roll this paper around it. It helps if you put a little oil on the skewer so the inside of this little bundle doesn't stick permanently. As you roll you can continue the incantation or make up another chant that more specifically illustrates your goal. Since we were talking about love, your paper could be colored red or pink, dabbed with rose oil, and the incantation might go like this:

> *Round and round, love abounds*
> *Without and within, this magick begins!*

Let the glue dry completely, then you can remove the bead and string it. Keep this for hanging off a rearview mirror, carrying in your pocket, burning in a ritual fire, for tossing into water, for burying in earth, and so forth as the need arises. Just make sure you keep track of each bead's purpose (try color coding them for ease—like green for prosperity and money, yellow for communication, and blue for happiness).

Final Words

I've really enjoyed visiting with you in the pages of this book. It's been a chance to share a little of my experiences, humor, and insights, with people that I hope will find them helpful. Even as a Cunning Woman, I am but one person—who tries to walk the walk with as much light as I have. Please know that my way is not the only way to approach magick and spirituality. It is simply what works for me. If you can find a little glimmer of something in these pages that also works for you, all the better. Happiness is something that grows when it's shared.

If you find you have questions that were not covered in this book, feel free to e-mail me at Granny@loresinger.com. I'll get back to you as soon as possible with whatever help I can offer. Be well, be blessed and BE the magick.

Select Bibliography

Aldington, Richard, trans. *New Larousse Encyclopedia of Mythology.* Middlesex, England: Hamlyn Publishing, 1973.

Ann, Martha, and Imel, Dorothy Myers. *Goddesses in World Mythology.* New York: Oxford University Press, 1995.

Beyerl, Paul. *Herbal Magick.* Custer, Wash.: Phoenix Publishing, 1998.

Bruce-Mitford, Miranda. *Illustrated Book of Signs & Symbols.* New York: DK Publishing, 1996.

Buckland, Raymond. *Advanced Candle Magick.* St. Paul, Minn.: Llewellyn Publications, 1996.

Budge, E. A. Wallis. *Amulets & Superstitions,* Oxford, England: Oxford University Press, 1930.

Cavendish, Richard. *A History of Magic.* New York: Taplinger Publishing, 1979.

Cristiani, R. S. *Perfumery and Kindred Arts.* Philadelphia: Baird and Company, 1877.

Cunningham, Scott. *Crystal, Gem, and Metal Magic.* St. Paul, Minn.: Llewellyn Publications, 1995.

——————. *Encyclopedia of Magical Herbs.* St. Paul, Minn.: Llewellyn Publications, 1988.

——————. *Magic in Food.* St. Paul, Minn: Llewellyn Publications, 1991.

Davison, Michael Worth, ed. *Everyday Life Through the Ages,* Pleasantville, N.Y.: Reader's Digest Association Ltd., 1992.

Farrar, Jane and Stewart. *Spells and How they Work.* Custer, Wash.: Phoenix Publishing, 1990.

Freethy, Ron. *From Agar to Zenru: A Book of Plant Uses, Names, and Folklore.* Chicago: Fromm International Publishing, 1985.

Gordon, Leslie. *Green Magic.* New York: Viking Press, 1977.

Gordon, Stuart. *Encyclopedia of Myths and Legends.* London: Headline Publishing, 1993.

Hall, Manley P. *Secret Teachings of All Ages.* San Francisco: Philosophical Research Society, 1977.

Hanh, Thich Nhat; *The Heart of the Buddha's Teaching.* New York: Broadway Books, 1999.

Harner, Michael. *The Way of the Shaman.* New York: Harper Collins, 1990.

Hutchinson, Ruth. *Every Day's a Holiday.* New York: Harper and Brothers, 1961.

Kunz, George Frederick. *Curious Lore of Precious Stones.* New York: Dover Publications, 1971.

Leach, Maria, ed. *Standard Dictionary of Folklore, Mythology, and Legend.* New York: Harper & Row, 1984.

Loewe, Michael, and Blacker, Carmen, eds. *Oracles and Divination.* Boulder, Colo.: Shambhala, 1981.

McArthur, Margie. *The Wisdom of the Elements.* Freedom, Calif.: Crossing Press, 1998.

Miller, Gustavus H. *Ten Thousand Dreams Interpreted.* Chicago: M. A. Donohuse & Co., 1931.

Oesterley, W.O.E. *The Sacred Dance.* Brooklyn, N.Y.: Dance Horizons, 1923.

Opie, Iona, and Tatem, Moira. *A Dictionary of Superstitions.* New York: Oxford University Press, 1989.

Potterton, D. ed. *Culpeper's Herbal.* New York: Sterling Publishing, 1983.

Telesco, Patricia: *Futuretelling.* Freedom, Calif.: Crossing Press, 1997.

——————. *Herbal Arts.* Secaucus, N.J.: Citadel Books, 1997.

——————. *Kitchen Witch's Cookbook.* St. Paul, Minn.: Llewellyn Publications, 1994.

——————. *Spinning Spells: Weaving Wonders.* Freedom, Calif.: Crossing Press, 1996.

Walker, Barbara. *The Woman's Dictionary of Symbols and Sacred Objects.* San Francisco: Harper & Row, 1988.

Waring, Philippa. *The Dictionary of Omens and Superstitions.* Secaucus, N.J.: Chartwell Books, 1978.

Index